Winners and Losers
in Colombia's
Economic Growth
of the 1970s

A WORLD BANK PUBLICATION

Winners and Losers in Colombia's Economic Growth of the 1970s

Miguel Urrutia

Published for The World Bank
OXFORD UNIVERSITY PRESS

Oxford University Press

NEW YORK OXFORD LONDON GLASGOW
TORONTO MELBOURNE WELLINGTON HONG KONG
TOKYO KUALA LUMPUR SINGAPORE JAKARTA
DELHI BOMBAY CALCUTTA MADRAS KARACHI
NAIROBI DAR ES SALAAM CAPE TOWN

First printing January 1985

EDITOR   Emmanuel D'Silva
PRODUCTION   Yamile M. Kahn
BOOK DESIGN   Yamile M. Kahn
FIGURES   S. A. D. Subasinghe
COVER DESIGN   Joyce C. Eisen

Library of Congress Cataloging in Publication Data

Urrutia, Miguel.
    Winners and losers in Colombia's economic growth of
the 1970s.

    Bibliography: p.
    Includes index.
    1. Colombia—Economic policy. 2. Income distribution—
Colombia. I. Title.
HC197.U789 1984   339.2'2'09861   84-12539
ISBN 0-19-520468-9

Contents

Foreword

SOCIAL SCIENTISTS HAVE HAD A DIFFICULT TIME fitting Colombian development experience of the past thirty years into fashionable categories such as
monetarism, structuralism, bureaucratic-authoritarianism, and such. Here is
another Latin American country without price stability, but where annual
inflation has seldom gone above 35 percent. This is a nation with import
and exchange controls, but where the extremes of South American
protectionism have been avoided. Colombia does not allow its peso to float
freely, but its crawling peg keeps it not too far from reasonable levels. Direct
foreign investment is welcome, but selectively. Colombia has not launched
grand social experiments, but its health and education indicators show
steady improvements. Faced by this disconcerting eclecticism, too many
international social scientists have ignored Colombia.

That the eclectic Colombian eystem has, for nearly thirty years,
generated significant and steady growth while maintaining a reasonably
democratic society seems to have decreased its appeal both to those
fascinated by socialist revolutions and to those impatient for a restoration
of pure laissez-faire in the economic sphere. Neither righteous European
socialists nor eminent North American professors feel compelled to study
(for two weeks) the Colombian case firsthand. Mercifully, the international
press carries no articles about a Colombian miracle. It is a safe bet that *either*
the Allende or the Pinochet administration in Chile has generated more
pages in international journals than fifty years of Colombian growth. When
the Colombian experience is brought up in learned symposia, it is more
likely to be dismissed with a silly-clever remark about drugs than discussed
seriously. Colombians, quite wisely, enjoy their solitude.

Miguel Urrutia is one of the few scholars who has offered the international academic community systematic and balanced analyses of Colombian development. With this book he does it again, this time challenging the notion (prejudice?) that Colombian growth during the 1970s served *only* to make the rich richer. He plunges into the tricky area of income distribution, unfazed by data problems, and sorts out with aplomb the bits and pieces of available evidence. His superb knowledge of Colombia and his analytical skills add weight to his cautious conclusions that in fact overall income distribution may have improved at the end of the 1970s, and that the 1970s appear to have witnessed a reduction in Colombian absolute poverty. His plausible conjecture that the Colombian democratic system may have had something to do with those two trends will not be popular among those who sneer at "bourgeois reformism" nor among those whose dogma is that politics can only worsen market outcomes.

Students of long-term development will find Urrutia's book most useful. Those anguished by the melancholy picture offered by Latin American economic performance and prospects during the early 1980s may take comfort in the long view offered by this volume. While avoiding the spectacular crises found elsewhere in Latin America, thanks largely to fairly prudent management, Colombian development has been negatively influenced by the bad news coming from abroad, especially from its immediate neighbors. At a time when the international economic system seems bent on rewarding political submission more than prudent economic management, Colombia faces difficult tradeoffs between austerity and autonomy. A serene reading of Urrutia's volume will offer an authoritative reminder that achieving both growth and the reduction of poverty, while maintaining national autonomy, is something Colombian policymakers have been able to do in the past and can continue to do in the future.

CARLOS F. DIAZ ALEJANDRO
Columbia University

September 1984

Preface

THIS BOOK IS THE RESULT of a collaborative effort among various researchers connected with Fedesarrollo, a private nonprofit research institute in Bogota, Colombia. A good part of the research was financed by the World Bank, but the last phase of preparation was possible thanks to the time the United Nations University allowed me to take away from my duties as vice rector for development studies at its headquarters in Tokyo.

Clara Elsa de Sandoval, an old friend who was my research assistant in my previous book on income distribution in Colombia, helped me to calculate the rural income distribution trends. Mauricio Carrizosa analyzed poverty levels, based on data from household surveys, and Martha de Higuera and Maria del Rosario Sintes helped put together the data on wages by occupation. Hernando Gomez Duque managed the data and the field work for the Cali survey of rich and poor families. Finally, Rakesh Mohan and Alvaro Pachon kindly made available much valuable data from their own research projects.

That the book is better than the first draft is largely due to the thoughtful comments of the anonymous peer reviewers assigned by the World Bank. They made me work hard to produce the revised version, but it was worth it. Finally, I am grateful for the comments and support of Fred Jaspersen, Nicholas Carter, and Guy Pfeffermann.

Because I am old-fashioned, I still write in longhand. My secretaries, Arcelia Ramirez, Yoshie Sawada, and Akiko Hara, have been very patient and helpful.

My only regret is that the deep economic crisis of the early 1980s will make it necessary for me to reexamine the income distribution trends in Colombia to see whether the improvements in income distribution registered in the late 1970s have continued into the new decade. For the first time in Colombian postwar history, the nation has had three years in a row of low economic growth, and the impact of this disaster on income distribution is not clear. The very rich have not done well since 1980, and many of the owners of the new financial groups are now in jail or in exile, having been able to take little money with them. Profits are down and many industries have gone broke. Unfortunately, the situation for the poor is not good either. Rural real wages have stopped increasing and unemployment is up. But since the inflation rate has come down, some real wages have increased. Consequently, it is difficult to tell what has happened to income distribution as a whole. In this book I analyze the trends in income distribution during a period of rapid economic growth. Toward 1986, I will have to analyze what happened to Colombia when economic stagnation set in.

MIGUEL URRUTIA

September 1984

Winners and Losers
in Colombia's
Economic Growth
of the 1970s

1

Introduction

COLOMBIA EXPERIENCED SUBSTANTIAL ECONOMIC GROWTH during the decade of the 1970s, but the question of who has benefited from this growth is the subject of some discussion. The weight of opinion is that the growth in the 1970s did not help the poor or improve the distribution of income. This study examines a wide array of data and arrives at a different conclusion—namely, that the income distribution did not deteriorate and that the real incomes of the poorest workers did, in fact, improve significantly during the decade.

An examination of who wins and who loses when a developing country experiences economic growth is always important. It is also appropriate for Colombia for two reasons. First, two governments in the 1970s—the administrations of Misael Pastrana (1970–74) and of Alfonso Lopez Michelsen (1974–78)—followed policies specifically designed to improve the distribution of income. Second, the democratic nature of Colombia's political institutions should help eliminate biases toward income concentration.

Pessimistic Opinions

Many informed people in Colombia believe, however, that the recent experience of economic growth has not clearly benefited the lower-income families. A few sample statements will illustrate this. In September 1980, the Colombian weekly *Consigna* characterized the country's development process as follows:

> For the Colombian people—except the elite—the decade from 1970 to 1980 was a bad experience: the quality of life did not improve; disparities among regions and between urban and rural areas widened; child labor was an appalling phenomenon; and the middle class was proletarianized

3

because of the worsening situation of the white-collar workers. These are the conclusions reached by one of the most respected research institutes in the country, under the direction of the National Association of Financial Institutions (ANIF).[1]

In May 1980, the liberal newspaper *El Tiempo* summarized the introduction of a new book by Senator Hernando Agudelo Villa, an ideologist of the left wing of the Liberal party, in which he states:

> The social situation in Colombia is more distressing and unfortunate every day because economic growth has not meant a growing and equitable improvement for the low-income sectors of the population, because inflation has deteriorated real wages, and because the phenomenon of a bad distribution of income has become more clear.[2]

Even the major employer federations seem to be concerned about the problem of a deteriorating income distribution. In April 1981, five major employer pressure groups drafted a joint document in which they criticized the government's economic policy. The document stated that "in relative terms, the growth of the economy in the 1970s produced results unfavorable to the low and middle classes."[3]

In general, academic opinion concurs. In 1981, J. A. Bejarano argued that the deterioration in income distribution that began in 1970 continued until the end of the decade.[4] Foreign economists agree. Albert Berry and Ronald Soligo, in their 1980 study, assert: "The tentative judgement must be that inequality has increased during the 1970s, and possibly during the late 1970s as well."[5] This finding has profound policy implications, especially in view of the fact that the authors begin their book by stating:

> Ironically, inequality increased in Colombian society precisely when those responsible for economic policy began to take a more direct interest in the problem of income distribution. Both the Pastrana and Lopez administrations formulated and carried out at least some policies whose purpose was to improve the distribution of income. Yet most of the empirical evidence suggests that income distribution worsened in the 1970s.[6]

This statement would suggest that government efforts to improve distribution have not been effective.

Methods and Conclusions of This Study

Fortunately, the Colombian data do not support such a pessimistic opinion. First of all, distribution policies were given varying degrees of emphasis in the two administrations mentioned earlier. These policies

clearly were more important in the Lopez Michelsen administration than
under Pastrana. Furthermore, redistribution policies in the fields of
education, health, nutrition, foreign trade policy, financial policy, and fiscal
policy cannot yield results in the short run. Therefore, assessing the impact
of policies put into effect in 1974 on the basis of 1975 data—the most
recent statistics available to Berry and Soligo when they published their
study—may not be methodologically correct.

Second, a complete analysis of all the existing statistical data shows that
the income distribution did not worsen in the 1970s and that the real
incomes of the poor improved significantly, especially in the latter half of
the decade.

The reason the results of this study differ so much from the opinion of
many observers is that the most commonly available statistics suggest a
process of income concentration. National income data on salaries and
statistics on real industrial wages show little improvement in an economy
with rapidly growing income per capita. This seems to suggest a worsening
of the relative income position of labor. A simple comparison of income
distribution derived from labor force surveys suggests the same thing.

Gustav Ranis, for example, in a 1980 study analyzes income survey data
and, on the basis of the distributions derived from these surveys for various
years, concludes that there has been some income concentration throughout the Colombian development process. Although he warns about the
quality of the data, he uses the survey information without adjustments to
arrive at conclusions on income distribution trends. He believes that "some
deterioration can be seen prior to the early 1960s, followed by a slight
improvement in the late 1960s and early 1970s, with a new worsening trend
thereafter."[7]

But the income data for Colombia used by Ranis and others are
incomplete and of highly variable quality. This means the estimates of
income distribution are not comparable and, therefore, cannot be used to
estimate changes in the indexes of concentration over time. Instead, a
detailed analysis must be made of the coverage and the quality of the
surveys used to obtain the primary income data, and a decision must then
be made on which information is comparable.

Chapter 4 of this study follows such a methodology. I first analyze the
quality and the coverage of the various household surveys and then
compare the income distribution derived from similar surveys. These
comparisons do not support the hypothesis of a worsening income
distribution.

To complement the analysis based on income surveys and censuses, it is
advisable also to analyze the information on earnings obtained from
periodic surveys of salaries and wages. This latter analysis should not,

however, be limited to wages in the manufacturing sector. This sector clearly generates the most abundant and best-known statistics, but it is highly probable that trends in manufacturing wages do not coincide with those in other sectors.

Accordingly, in Chapter 2, the present study uses various wage series as a complement to analyses of changes in distribution based on data obtained from household income surveys. These data also do not reflect a worsening of the distribution. The real wages of the very poor—the landless agricultural laborers—increased rapidly in the decade, as did the wages of various categories of unskilled urban workers. The sluggish trend of real wages in large manufacturing establishments and among white-collar workers is therefore not typical. Furthermore, all the data point to little growth in real income for the poor in the first part of the decade and to rapid progress in their standard of living in the second part of the decade, after economic policy started to be consciously designed with distributional goals in mind.

Income surveys and wage series show average conditions and changes for different categories of the population, but they do not show what has happened to the real incomes and to the economic welfare of families and individuals over time. For that reason, an attempt is made in Chapter 3 to follow the fortunes of a group of poor families in Cali through the entire decade. The real incomes for this sample of poor families increased by about 100 percent in the decade.

Obtaining information on the wealthiest group of the income distribution is difficult. On the basis of the survey conducted in Cali, however, and a comparison of the rates of increase in the incomes of the poor and the middle class relative to the national per capita income, it can be concluded that the richest 5 percent of the families certainly did not suffer any loss in their share of the national income during the last two decades. But it is also possible that this share did not increase as much as is commonly believed.

In Chapter 5 an effort is made to measure the proportion of families in absolute poverty at various times during the decade. This exercise again shows a deteriorating situation in the first part of the decade and clear improvements after 1976. It thus appears that different sets of data provide a fairly consistent picture of short-term changes in income distribution, and none of the data sets used confirm a deterioration in income distribution during the 1970s.

In Chapter 6 I suggest some hypotheses that may explain why income distribution did not become less equal in the decade, and discuss some policy implications of the Colombian growth experience of the 1970s. This last chapter is tentative, because the main objective of this stage of my research was to find out what had really happened with the income distribution in Colombia between 1965 and 1980.

In summary, the main finding of this study is that in the decade and a half after 1964, income distribution in the country did not deteriorate, and the real income of the poorest families increased significantly. Many people have criticized the economic policies followed in the 1970s, asserting that they led to a worsening of the income distribution and did not benefit the poor. The data collected here suggest the contrary: that if economic policy had an impact on distribution, it was to favor the poor.

It is possible, however, that factors other than official economic policy, such as high coffee prices and the rapid growth of coffee production, helped to avoid a deterioration in income distribution. Nevertheless, a case can be made for the hypothesis that official policies helped to channel some of the incomes from the export boom of the late 1970s toward low-income families. There is no question, however, that exogenous factors, such as decreasing rates of population growth and the adoption of new technology in agriculture, affected distribution significantly. This study does not try to determine how each of these phenomena and each policy affected income distribution.

From a historical perspective, the finding that a resource-rich country that followed fairly orthodox economic policies in the 1970s was able to achieve rapid growth, with no deterioration in income distribution and without increasing its foreign debt, may be both unexpected and significant.

Notes to Chapter 1

1. *Consigna*, September 15, 1980.
2. *El Tiempo*, May 10, 1980, p. 15A.
3. ANDI (Asociacion Nacional de Industriales), ANIF (Asociacion Nacional de Instituciones Financieras), CAMACOL (Camara Colombiana de la Construccion), FEDEMETAL (Federacion Metalurgica Nacional), and FENALCO (Federacion Nacional de Comerciantes), "Documento Dirigido al Presidente de la Republica," April 1981.
4. J. A. Bejarano, "Crecimiento, Distribucion y Politica Economica" (Paper presented to the Congreso de Economistas de la Universidad Nacional, Melgar, May 1980; processed).
5. Albert Berry and Ronald Soligo, *Economic Policy and Income Distribution in Colombia* (Boulder: Westview Press, 1980), p. 17.
6. Ibid., p. 1.
7. Gustav Ranis, "Distribucion del Ingreso y Crecimiento en Colombia," *Desarrollo y Sociedad*, no. 3 (January 1980).

2

Changes in Incomes
of Different Occupations

ONE USEFUL WAY TO EXAMINE CHANGES in income distribution over time is
to compare the trends in wages for workers in different occupations. This
type of analysis gives some idea of the changing income of populations with
different skill levels and demographic characteristics. Also, because such
analysis identifies variations in income differentials among large groups of
the population, it may enable one to recognize broad transformations in
social structure. Furthermore, the data on incomes by occupation are often
of better quality than the data from household surveys used to calculate
general measures of inequality; this is so because wage data are often based
on the accounting records of enterprises, whereas survey data are based on
the general impression of a respondent (usually a housewife) on the
income of various household members. Of course, wage data are not useful
for analyzing trends in capital income, which in general applies to the
wealthiest group in society. But if one is interested in seeing what has
happened to the poor, wage series are a good starting point. This is
particularly true if it can be shown that differentials in labor income
between wage earners and independent workers of the same age and sex
and with similar education are not large; and this seemed to be the case in
Colombia in the 1970s.

The Poor in the Rural Sector

In 1964, Colombia's poorest group of workers were the landless rural
laborers. Daily farm wages were much lower than the wages earned by any
urban worker. Wages of unskilled workers in construction were 10 percent
higher than agricultural wages in 1964, while the wages of blue-collar
industrial workers were three times higher (see Table 1). Moreover, rural

Table 1. *Trends in Average Daily Wages for Various Occupational Categories*
(constant 1954 Colombian pesos)

Year	Agricultural workers[a]	Unskilled construction workers		Unskilled and semiskilled construction workers in four cities[d]	Manufacturing industry workers	
		Bogota[b]	Four cities[c]		Blue-collar[e]	White-collar[e]
1960	3.35	4.08	—	—	8.55	25.82
1961	3.53	4.08	—	—	—	26.09
1962	3.82	4.28	—	—	11.41	27.41
1963	3.86	4.08	—	—	12.23	27.09
1964	3.89	4.28	—	—	11.82	26.64
1965	3.87	4.64	—	—	12.23	27.55
1966	3.88	4.00	—	—	11.91	26.95
1967	3.82	4.40	—	—	12.18	27.73
1968	3.76	4.68	—	—	12.50	28.64
1969	4.03	—	—	—	12.82	30.18
1970	3.90	4.64	—	—	13.82	34.09
1971	3.72	4.28	—	5.99	13.55	33.64
1972	—	4.70	4.61	5.64	1.314	32.27
1973	—	4.40	4.24	5.23	12.05	30.27
1974	—	4.50	4.33	5.26	11.45	28.73

1975	—	4.50	4.70	4.84	11.23	28.09
1976	4.75	4.39	4.60	5.15	11.50	28.00
1977	5.34	4.25	4.40	4.88	10.86	26.23
1978	5.83	4.81	5.00	5.68	12.05	27.41
1979	5.79	5.34	5.50	6.43	12.86	27.86

—Data not available.

Note: Deflators: In all cases, cost-of-living indexes of blue-collar workers will normally be used to deflate wage rates. For national wage series, the national index was used, while for city wages, the index for that city was used. Daily wages are compared to avoid overestimations or underestimations in the case of agricultural and construction workers, who are not paid monthly and who normally do not work the entire month.

a. Cold and hot regions were weighted equally. For 1960–71, the figure is the daily wage of males, without food. For 1976–79, it is the daily agricultural wage without food.

b. For 1960–71, the table shows the series of wages paid to helpers in a small construction firm. For 1972–79, the figure is the average wage for helpers, based on the index published by DANE for Bogota.

c. Weighted average of the wage paid to helpers in Bogota, Medellin, Cali, and Barranquilla. Assumes the following weights: 55 percent for Bogota, 20 percent for Medellin, 19 percent for Cali, and 6 percent for Barranquilla.

d. Weighted average of wages paid to journeymen and helpers in Bogota, Medellin, Cali, and Barranquilla. A weight of 55 percent was assigned to the wage of helpers and 45 percent to that of journeymen.

e. Assumes twenty-two days of work a month.

Source: Departamento Administrativo Nacional de Estadística (DANE).

laborers had benefited little from national economic growth during the three previous decades. The available statistics suggest that between 1935 and 1964 the purchasing power of agricultural workers earning daily wages did not increase.

In 1964, the majority of the poor were in the rural sector. For that year, the average income of an employed person in the seventh decile of the rural population was less than the average income of an employed person in the second decile of the urban population. Put in another way, 71 percent of the economically active people with incomes of less than 3,400 pesos per year in 1964 lived in the rural area, and this included 58 percent of the rural labor force.[1] Clearly, not all of this large number of rural poor were workers on daily wages. Owners of small farms who derived an important part of their income from work outside their farms also had very low incomes.

Rural poverty, of course, is not confined to Colombia. In most of the developing countries, poverty, underemployment, and even malnutrition are concentrated in the rural sector. In fact, the development process consists precisely in the creation of remunerative employment outside agriculture and in the improvement of the productivity of agricultural workers. Only when the rural population ceases to grow in absolute terms—because of a decline in the rural birth rate and the absorption of the increase in the rural labor force by sectors other than agriculture—can the real incomes of rural workers be expected to begin rising.

W. Arthur Lewis's model of a dual economy implies stagnation of agricultural daily wages in real terms as long as there is redundant labor in the countryside.[2] According to this model, agricultural wages can increase in real terms only when the excess supply of rural labor has been absorbed; this probably occurs when the rural population ceases to grow or begins to decline. Historical experience seems to confirm this type of model. Ohkawa and Ranis, for example, show that in Japan agricultural wages did not begin to rise significantly until after 1917, when the agricultural labor force began to fall in absolute terms.[3]

Furthermore, a number of researchers have concluded that income distribution in developing countries begins to improve only when there is no more excess labor.[4] For this reason, income distribution in the Republic of Korea and in Taiwan, where nonagricultural employment has expanded rapidly, is better than the average for economies with a similar level of per capita income. Thus, it is important to analyze the movement of agricultural wages in Colombia: an increase in those wages might reflect a decline in underemployment, and therefore the beginning of a development phase in which income distribution could improve.

Data from Colombia's Departmento Administrativo Nacional de Estadistica (DANE) show a slight upward trend in real agricultural wages during the 1950s and 1960s and a more substantial improvement in the late 1970s. Figure 1 shows the trend for agricultural wages for males between 1945 and 1971, in four departments (provinces) and in the nation as a whole. Antioquia and Caldas, both coffee-producing areas, were high-wage departments in the 1940s, and Antioquia had experienced some industrialization by that time. Boyaca and Nariño, by contrast, were both poor rural areas, but Boyaca, because it was close to Bogota, was influenced by the rapid urban growth of the capital city. On the semilogarithmic scale, the slope of the curve for Antioquia, the most industrialized area in 1948, is near zero until 1970; for Nariño and Boyaca, the two departments with the lowest wage levels at the start, the slope is positive, but, for Caldas, it is less so. The higher rates of growth for Boyaca and Nariño suggest a small decrease in the amount of excess labor in these two highly populated and poor departments during this period.

Table 2 displays the annual average rate of change in real agricultural wages for the nation and for the seven departments; it also compares these with rates of change in national per capita income. The table shows that between 1953 and 1969 agricultural wages increased at about the same rate as national per capita income, which means that rural workers roughly maintained their relative position in the income distribution.[5] Since the rate of change of income per employed worker is higher than the per capita figure—because the population grew faster than the labor force—rural workers probably had a slightly lower share of total income in 1969 than in 1953. After 1970, agricultural laborers probably improved their relative position, particularly when one considers that the labor force grew more rapidly than the total population. This means that the agricultural wage with no food provided, shown in Table 1, grew roughly as fast as national income per worker. The agricultural wage with food provided, which appears on Table 2, grew much faster than national income per worker.

Unfortunately, DANE discontinued its statistics on agricultural wages in 1969 (those for 1970 and 1971 are estimates). It did not resume its survey until 1976, and the new series uses a slightly different methodology. As Figure 1 shows, the 1976 wage level is significantly higher than that of 1969. The question, therefore, arises whether the higher level was due merely to the change in the sample, or whether it reflects a real improvement in the standard of living of rural workers.

Analysis of the methodology used for the two series leads to the conclusion that they are not very different. The series ending in 1969 showed the "maximum," "minimum," and "most frequent" wage paid in each municipality, based on information provided by a well-informed person in that municipality. The departmental wage was the most commonly observed of the most frequent wages for the municipalities in

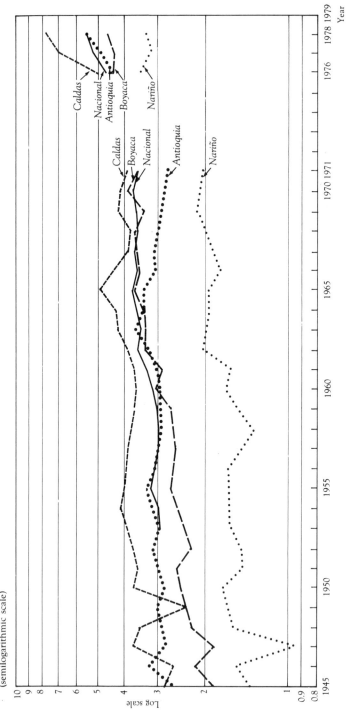

Figure 1. *Trends in Real Agricultural Wages for Males in Colombia, 1948–79* (semilogarithmic scale)

Note: These figures are for wages without food in four cold-climate departments and in the nation as a whole. The semilogarithmic scale shows rates of growth.

Source: Departamento Administrativo Nacional de Estadística (DANE).

14

Table 2. *Annual Average Rate of Change of Real Agricultural Wages*
(percent)

Department	1953–69 [a]	1953–77 [b]	1960–69 [a]	1964–79 [b]	1969–76 [c]	1969–76 [b]	1976–79 [d]
National	1.52	3.47	1.49	4.60	4.43	6.66	12.02
Antioquia	-0.32	3.09	-0.75	4.63	6.63	8.80	14.03
Boyaca	2.88	4.03	1.84	3.98	6.06	5.89	5.47
Caldas	-0.18	2.86	—	4.05	4.75	7.92	15.70
Magdalena	4.41	3.75	7.74	4.08	-1.14	2.70	12.29
Nariño	1.76	3.72	2.26	5.27	8.15	6.94	4.18
Santander	1.23	2.40	0.36	2.31	3.86	4.31	5.37
Valle	-0.31	2.39	0.28	3.46	4.52	6.86	12.50
Rate of change of per capita income	1.59	2.50	2.72	3.67	4.10	4.12	4.19

—Data not available.

Note: The rate of change is calculated by solving for I in the formula $VF = VP (1 + i)^n$, where i = rate of growth per year of the series, VF = wage in the last year, VP = wage in the first year, and n = number of years. The figures for the series through 1969 refer to the wages of males. All figures are for cold climate with food supplied. The table includes different periods to allow the reader to see rates of growth for the whole period and also for each of the wage series, since it may be that they are not comparable.

a. DANE wage series, old methodology.
b. Wage series constructed from the two different DANE sets.
c. Change between the two DANE wage series.
d. DANE wage series, new methodology.

that department. The series beginning in 1976 is based on information from the Caja Agraria (an agricultural bank) on the most frequent wages in each municipality, but the departmental wage is the average of the most frequent wages paid in the municipalities.[6] The second series includes wages in both farming and stockraising, but eliminates the distinction between wages of males and those of females.

Because the dispersion of the "most frequent wages" by municipality tends to be slight, the average wage and the most frequent wage by province are probably similar. In theory, because of greater dispersion, the difference between the two wages could be greater for the national figures, but Figure 1 does not show an unreasonable growth of national wages compared with wages in the selected provinces. The methodological changes in the two wage series would, therefore, appear not to be so fundamental as to prevent their comparison.[7] Nonetheless, because the increase from the end of one series to the beginning of the other is significant, an effort was made to obtain independent wage data for 1969–76 to verify whether the increase was real.[8]

Data collected from the books of a few farms confirm the trends shown in Table 2. Real agricultural wages on farms in Boyaca and Cundinamarca increased substantially between 1969 and 1976, while the rate of growth was low or negative for farms in Valle. Table 2 also shows that rural wages grew faster in Boyaca than in Valle. Nevertheless, the direct farm data are too scanty to confirm or contradict the hypothesis that real rural wages grew during the period DANE discontinued its survey. More wage series from individual farms would have to be reconstructed to fill the gap in DANE wage information during 1969–76.

What is clear is that since 1976 the incomes of rural workers have risen significantly; this is shown in both the DANE series and the data from individual farms. Between 1976 and 1979, agricultural wages in the country rose three times faster than national per capita income: the national farm wage index rose by 12 percent, while the national per capita income index rose by only 4 percent. Thus, in the second half of the 1970s, the income differential between rural and urban workers declined. In other words, the poorest group of workers in the society increased its standard of living more than the average. However, the increase in farm wages in the two poorest departments—Boyaca and Nariño—was much lower than the national index.

Figure 1 reflects several other phenomena that deserve mention. First, the large increases in farm wages in Caldas and Antioquia, beginning in 1976, may bear some relation to increases in coffee production. Second, the data from farms suggest that during the 1970s wages increased less in departments where they were already high, such as in Valle. Third, the rural minimum wage has increased rapidly since 1973, and it may be that this has contributed to raising the level of real wages. The farm data show that wages paid tend to increase when the minimum wage is raised.

In addition to wages, the number of days worked also affects the incomes of rural laborers. Because of Colombia's topography, regions, sometimes fairly close to each other, experience peaks in labor demand at different times of the year, and there is evidence of much short-term geographical mobility of rural labor as a result. The improvements in communications have probably led to an increase in the number of days worked per year. At present, however, there is no empirical evidence on changes in the number of days worked.

According to economic theory, changes in the minimum wage can increase the income of workers when monopsony conditions are present. These conditions are possible in the rural sector, where a few landowners can set the level of wages for their workers. In this case, an increase in the real minimum wage—as long as it is not so high as to cause unemployment—could reduce the profits of the landowner and increase the earnings of the worker. Thus, one cannot reject the hypothesis that increases in the real minimum wage could have contributed to the rapid increases in real wages. In fact, the data from individual farms show that in general the minimum wage legislation has been effective. These data show that in all cases during 1975–79, the wages of unskilled workers, who often earn the minimum wage, increased more than those of overseers and skilled workers. This phenomenon, however, is consistent with a general decrease in wage differentials between skilled and unskilled workers observed at all levels of the economy. It is, therefore, likely that factors other than the minimum wage legislation were affecting the income of unskilled rural workers.

The rural minimum wage in real terms increased 35 percent between November 1974 and January 1980. If there had not been some labor scarcity, such an increase in minimum wage would have led employers not to comply with the minimum wage legislation; there is no evidence that this occurred. Given the weak bargaining power of individual rural workers, what probably happened was that the minimum wage legislation accelerated wage adjustments that would have taken place more gradually. The government, pressured by the unions, proposed large increases in rural minimum wages, which the modern sector farmers did not oppose at the bargaining table because they had to pay wages higher than the minimum wage to keep their laborers. This raised the wages of laborers working in smaller and more traditional farms. At the end of the decade, when minimum wages started approaching market wages on modern farms, pressure by employers against continued increases in rural minimum wages by the Salary Council intensified; thereafter, increases in real rural wages became much less rapid. Minimum wage management, therefore, may have had some influence on the income of some rural workers.

The increase in real agricultural wages during the 1970s may mark the beginning of an improvement in the standard of living of the poorest groups in Colombian society. Not only did the wages of farm workers increase, but most likely so did the incomes of small landowners because many of them are also daily workers. In fact, stagnation in the incomes of small rural landowners is incompatible with significant increases in agricultural wages; otherwise the smallholder would become a daily worker. Because these two groups make up a significant proportion of the poor in Colombia, their economic improvement over the last decade has major implications for the national welfare.

Occupations of the Urban Poor

Myths abound concerning who are the poor in the cities of Colombia. Some believe that recent arrivals from rural areas constitute the largest group of urban poor. Many studies, however, have demonstrated that immigrants are not poorer than persons born in the city, nor do they face a greater likelihood of being unemployed.[9] Others believe that many of the poor are in the informal sector of the economy, defined as the group consisting of self-employed persons, employees of small enterprises, and workers in trade and services.

Mohan's 1980 study, however, shows that only construction workers and persons in domestic service are paid significantly less than workers in the manufacturing industry (see Table 3).

Unquestionably, construction workers are the most poorly paid urban group next only to those in domestic service. Unfortunately, official statistics of their income were not published before 1972, and, although Urrutia and Berry constructed a daily wage series based on official statistics, the data for the 1960s do not seem to be sufficiently reliable.[10] Accordingly, Fedesarrollo, a research institute, obtained wage series directly from two construction firms in Bogota (one small firm and one large organized firm) to compare the data with official figures for the 1970s. Table 4 shows the series of daily wages at constant 1954 prices for the two construction firms for 1959–79. Table 5 presents the DANE series for the total construction labor force and by skill categories for the 1970s.

Between 1960 and 1970, real wages for construction workers increased, according to both the series in Tables 1 and 4, but the increase was not constant. The real wage reached its highest level in the middle of the decade. In the 1970s, the daily wage (in Bogota, Medellin, and Cali) increased only at the end of the decade and concurrently with a decline in urban unemployment. In Barranquilla, however, the average wage in construction still has not regained its 1972 level, although the series shows an upward trend beginning in 1978. Since construction wages in Barranquilla were higher than those in other cities in 1972, labor mobility may explain why the wage decrease was so marked between that year and 1975. In general, the real wages of helpers and journeymen increased more than those of masters.

During both the 1960s and the 1970s, the daily wage of construction workers rose less than national per capita income, implying that workers in the construction sector lost out relative to other sectors. It is not certain, however, what happened to the annual income of construction workers in the 1970s. If the reduction in unemployment meant more days worked in a year, the rise in annual income would be greater than the increase in the daily wage. If the average period of employment did not increase, however, this means the real incomes of construction workers rose at an annual rate of only 2 percent during the decade, while national per capita income increased by about 3.5 percent. The Fedesarrollo data for the two firms in Bogota shows that the large firm had greater annual increases in labor cost than the smaller firm. When the two firms are weighted equally, however, the behavior of the average wage in Table 4 is similar to the DANE statistics in Table 5.

Within the construction industry during the 1970s, the salaries of helpers rose at a faster rate than those of masters and journeymen. This was true both for the large firm and for the weighted average of the two firms, as well as for the DANE figures for all cities except Barranquilla.

Over the two decades, the income differential between helpers and masters in the small firm dropped from 3.90 to 2.91, while that between masters and journeymen together and helpers decreased from 1.94 to 1.90. It can thus be concluded that the incomes of unskilled and semiskilled workers in construction rose more than the average for that sector. This phenomenon is found in most urban statistics. Moreover, it is consistent with the results of the analysis of poor and wealthy families in Cali presented in Chapter 3. That analysis shows that the incomes of secondary workers in poor families—who, like helpers in the construction industry, are generally young—have risen more rapidly than the incomes of primary workers.

Table 3. *Monthly Earnings and Distribution of Workers by Occupation in Bogota,*
1973 and 1977
(earnings in current Colombian pesos)

	1973					
	Males (M)		Females (F)		All	Earnings ratio
Occupation (ILO code)	Mean Y	Percent	Mean Y	Percent	(percent)	F/M
Professional and technical	6,090	8.3	2,740	8.0	8.2	0.45
(1-19)	(1.18)		(1.68)			
Administrative and manager	9,412	2.1	3,692	0.5	1.6	0.39
(20-29)	(0.98)		(1.03)			
Clerk and typist	2,136	10.3	1,760	17.4	12.7	0.82
(30-39)	(1.42)		(1.24)			
Sales managers and proprietors	3,338	7.8	1,736	3.8	6.5	0.52
(40-41)	(1.92)		(2.55)			
Other sales	2,059	8.6	743	7.9	8.4	0.36
(42-49)	(2.00)		(0.98)			
Service workers (excluding maids)	1,416	7.1	807	14.0	9.4	0.57
(50-53; 55-59)	(2.5)		(2.37)			
Maids	537	0.5	364	30.4	10.6	0.68
(54)	(0.90)		(1.64)			
Agriculture workers	2,698	1.9	3,032	0.2	1.3	1.13
(60-69)	(3.02)		(2.24)			
Production supervisors	1,325	5.1	851	3.5	4.6	0.64
(70)	(1.29)		(0.68)			
Production workers	1,279	27.2	810	14.1	22.7	0.63
(71-94; 96, 97)	(1.15)		(1.71)			
Construction workers	968	10.8	487	0.1	7.2	0.50
(95)	(1.29)		(0.83)			
Transport workers	1,389	8.3	1,408	0.0	5.5	1.01
(98)	(0.77)		(0.82)			
Other	701	2.1	597	0.0	1.4	0.85
	(0.73)		(0.70)			
Total	2,166	100.0	1,043	100.0	100.0	0.48
	(1.95)		(2.13)			
Number of workers (thousands)		436		223	659	
Number of workers responding in sample		37,455		17,456	53,911	
No information (percent)		12.0		12.42		

—Data not available.
n.s. Not significant.
Note: Coefficients of variation are in parentheses. Because of rounding, the percentage figures
may not correspond to the totals. Mean Y is mean income.

1977					
Males (M)		Females (F)		All (percent)	Earnings ratio F/M
Mean Y	Percent	Mean Y	Percent		
11,921 (0.87)	12.0	6,197 (0.87)	9.0	10.9	0.52
13,993 (0.69)	4.6	5,309 (0.47)	0.7	3.1	0.38
4,390 (0.87)	11.7	3,600 (0.55)	18.8	14.4	0.82
7,734 (1.22)	7.7	3,470 (1.68)	5.2	6.8	0.45
4,794 (1.10)	8.9	1,911 (1.09)	9.0	8.9	0.40
3,055 (0.63)	7.9	1,971 (0.97)	17.1	11.4	0.64
1,731 (0.30)	0.1	2,279 (0.32)	24.4	9.3	1.32
8,033 (1.20)	1.7	3,038 (1.34)	0.5	1.2	0.38
6,314 (0.92)	1.0	4,795 (0.50)	0.3	0.7	0.76
3,151 (1.37)	28.2	1,896 (0.60)	15.0	23.2	0.60
2,226 (0.62)	8.2	1,800 (0.0)	n.s.	5.1	0.81
3,558 (0.78)	7.5	— —	—	4.7	—
2,345 (0.41)	n.s.	n.s.	n.s.	0.4	—
5,402 (1.27)	100.0	2,828	100.0	100.0	0.52
	733		442	1,175	
	3,371		2,039	5,410	
	—		—	—	

Source: Rakesh Mohan, *The People of Bogota: Who They Are, What They Earn, Where They Live,* World Bank Staff Working Paper no. 390 (Washington, D.C., 1980). Data for 1973 are based on the population census sample and for 1977 on the EH-15 household survey.

Table 4. *Average Real Daily Wages in Two Construction Firms in Bogota, 1959–79*
(constant 1954 Colombian pesos)

Year	Small firm				Large firm				Weighted[a]			
	Helper	Journeyman	Master	Total[b]	Helper	Journeyman	Master	Total[b]	Helper	Journeyman	Master	Total[b]
1959	3.39	6.80	13.20	5.84	—	—	—	—	—	—	—	—
1960	4.06	6.53	12.67	5.90	—	—	—	—	—	—	—	—
1961	4.09	6.14	12.87	5.80	—	—	—	—	—	—	—	—
1962	4.28	6.16	14.27	6.10	—	—	—	—	—	—	—	—
1963	4.07	5.97	14.06	5.90	—	—	—	—	—	—	—	—
1964	4.26	6.25	14.70	6.20	—	—	—	—	—	—	—	—
1965	4.62	8.00	14.20	7.00	—	—	—	—	—	—	—	—
1966	4.00	6.89	14.81	6.30	—	—	—	—	—	—	—	—
1967	4.38	6.58	13.70	6.30	—	—	—	—	—	—	—	—
1968	4.66	7.77	12.94	6.80	—	—	—	—	—	—	—	—
1969	—c	—c	—c	—c	—	—	—	—	—	—	—	—

Year												
1970	4.62	6.60	14.30	6.40	—	—	—	—	—	—	—	—
1971	4.14	6.15	14.12	6.00	4.08	6.64	19.16	6.70	4.11	6.39	16.64	6.35
1972	5.21	7.15	17.65	7.30	4.20	6.52	18.52	6.60	4.70	6.83	18.08	6.90
1973	4.31	6.18	20.13	6.70	4.12	5.76	17.24	6.10	4.21	5.97	18.68	6.40
1974	4.91	6.36	17.34	6.80	4.44	6.12	18.04	6.50	4.67	6.24	17.69	6.60
1975	—c	—c	—c	—c	4.48	6.08	17.48	6.50	—	—	—	—
1976	3.99	5.40	12.53	5.40	4.64	6.36	17.60	6.70	4.31	5.88	15.06	6.00
1977	4.82	6.33	12.65	6.20	4.64	6.28	17.40	6.60	4.73	6.30	15.02	6.40
1978	5.13	7.96	15.40	7.40	5.40	7.44	20.04	7.70	5.26	7.70	17.72	7.60
1979[d]	5.30	8.18	15.47	7.60	5.84	7.40	20.92	8.00	5.57	7.79	18.19	7.70

—Data not available.

Note: Wages are deflated by the blue-collar consumer price index for Bogota: base 1954– 55 = 100.

a. Assuming equal participation for each of the two firms in the total.

b. The DANE weighting system was used (47 percent helper, 43 percent journeyman, and 10 percent master).

c. The small firm did no construction in that year.

d. For the small firm, the figure is the average for the first quarter; for the large firm, it is the average for January.

Source: Construction company records.

Table 5. *Average Real Daily Wages in the Construction Industry in Four Colombian Cities, by Category and Total, 1972–79*
(constant 1954 Colombian pesos)

City and category	1972	1973	1974	1975	1976	1977	1978	1979	Annual rate of change 1972–79 (percent)
Bogota									
Total	6.9	6.5	6.5	6.7	6.5	6.0	6.9	7.8	1.8
Master	18.6	18.2	18.7	18.1	16.4	15.2	17.6	18.3	-0.2
Journeyman	6.8	6.5	6.5	6.6	6.3	5.6	6.7	8.0	2.3
Helper	4.7	4.4	4.5	4.7	4.6	4.4	5.0	5.5	2.3
Medellin									
Total	6.2	5.7	5.6	5.7	5.6	5.5	6.5	7.1	1.9
Master	13.0	12.5	12.0	11.5	11.5	11.0	13.6	13.6	3.5
Journeyman	6.5	6.1	5.7	5.6	5.5	5.5	6.7	7.3	1.4
Helper	4.6	4.2	4.3	4.5	4.4	4.4	5.0	5.5	2.6
Cali									
Total	6.5	6.1	6.0	6.1	5.7	5.6	6.4	7.1	1.3
Master	22.0	19.7	18.3	17.1	14.6	13.9	15.7	15.9	-4.5
Journeyman	7.0	6.4	6.3	6.3	5.8	5.8	6.7	7.6	1.2
Helper	4.0	3.7	3.7	4.0	3.7	3.7	4.2	4.8	2.6
Barranquilla									
Total	7.9	7.2	7.1	6.0	6.3	5.9	6.8	7.1	
Master	13.4	12.3	13.1	12.3	12.6	12.1	17.7	14.3	0.9
Journeyman	8.7	7.1	8.1	6.4	6.6	6.1	7.3	7.6	-1.9
Helper	5.7	4.6	4.9	4.2	4.6	4.1	4.8	5.0	-1.8

Note: "Total" uses the DANE-weighted average for master, journeyman, and helper. The amount in pesos was calculated on the basis of the labor cost index of DANE, using average wages by category of personnel in each municipality for December 1979. In the total, weights of 10 percent, 43 percent, and 47 percent were assigned, respectively, to the three categories. These figures were then deflated by the blue-collar consumer price index for each city.

Source: DANE.

The DANE figures in Table 1 indicate that since the second half of the 1970s the agricultural wage has exceeded the wage of construction helpers in the four cities studied. In Cali, the agricultural wage was higher than the average wage for all construction workers in 1977 and 1978.[11]

Finally, data from the Social Security Institute (ISS) on insured persons working in construction indicates a reduction in real wages during 1972–76 and a rising trend in 1976–79. However, the absolute level of earnings in these data is much higher than the level reported by DANE and the sample of firms, because the persons covered are permanent employees of the construction companies and include white-collar workers, architects, and some older and well-trained workers. As a rule, laborers are hired by subcontractors and are not covered by social security.

In the case of services and trade, there are no official statistical series of wages covering at least a decade. Accordingly, a series had to be prepared on the basis of the records of selected firms. Table 6 presents information on wages for three retail trade stores—a supermarket, a parts store, and an appliance store. The data for the supermarket show gains in the real monthly wages of unskilled personnel, but the growth rate is lower than that of national per capita income. Between 1962 and 1978, the real incomes of cashiers rose at an average annual rate of 1.2 percent, those of packers did not rise, those of markers rose by 1.1 percent, and those of cutters rose by less than 1 percent a year. Thus, all of the groups lost out in relative terms.

Furthermore, there were significant increases during the 1960s and a real decline in the 1970s. Wages in the other stores in the table behaved similarly. Increases in real wages were small or nil during the 1970s, and in all cases were less than the rise in national per capita income. In retail trade, as in agriculture, construction, and services, wages increased more in the second part of the 1970s than in the first; in fact, from 1970 to 1975, real wages declined. Also in trade, as in construction and manufacturing, wage differentials by level of training narrowed over the decade.

DANE also has data on earnings in retail trade beginning in 1975. According to its sample, such earnings rose by 17 percent in real terms between 1975 and 1979, representing an average annual increase of 3.6 percent (see Table 7).

In the service sector, five firms—a restaurant, a laundry, two hotels, and a liquids-handling plant—were surveyed (see Table 8). The series for four of the firms show stagnation or very low growth in wages. They also indicate deterioration in the first part of the decade and an improvement beginning in 1974–75. The exception is the hotel in Girardot, which is more of a social club.

Table 6. *Average Real Monthly Wages Paid by Three Retail Trade Stores,*
1962–79
(constant 1954 Colombian pesos)

	Supermarket[a]				Parts store[b]		
Year	Cashier	Packer	Marker	Cutter	Salesman	Repairman	Secretary
1962	211	208	242	259	—	—	—
1963	249	220	249	246	—	—	—
1964	257	203	276	257	—	—	—
1965	267	214	288	266	—	—	—
1966	251	192	269	275	—	—	—
1967	255	192	285	304	—	—	—
1968	265	207	303	302	—	—	—
1969	264	212	306	289	—	—	—
1970	273	218	315	287	419	168	279
1971	281	204	328	279	383	191	298
1972	275	182	321	273	535	191	298
1973	252	151	289	250	238	111	222
1974	247	197	240	239	250	115	209
1975	240	191	279	260	266	131	208
1976	245	196	277	280	409	133	212
1977	232	185	262	260	387	168	215
1978	255	204	289	286	372	163	207
1979	—	—	—	—	327	190	233

—Data not available.

Note: Wages are deflated by the blue-collar and white-collar consumer price index for Bogota:
base 1954–55 = 100.

a. The figures correspond to the basic wage of a person holding the position in a large
supermarket chain in Bogota.

b. The data correspond to the basic wage for the position in a store in Boyaca with fewer than
ten employees.

	Appliance store[c]						
Watchman	Cleaner	Messenger	Technician	Cashier	Secretary	Manager[d]	Average[e]
—	—	—	—	—	—	—	—
—	—	—	—	—	—	—	—
—	—	—	—	—	—	—	—
—	—	—	—	—	—	—	—
—	—	—	—	—	—	—	—
—	—	—	—	—	—	—	—
—	—	—	—	—	—	—	—
—	—	—	—	—	—	—	—
154	181	132	374	219	264	753	275
170	181	131	343	235	272	928	294
158	176	141	318	247	265	946	291
153	153	144	345	216	244	819	269
144	156	162	347	208	266	901	284
142	138	170	331	216	239	784	269
157	155	158	376	227	223	831	277
150	149	149	386	257	221	895	266
150	164	155	321	236	241	930	279
188	193	169	388	252	285	878	300

c. The data correspond to the average basic wage for all identical positions in the Bogota branches of a large appliance store. Most of the positions have been held by the same persons, and for this reason the basic wage implicitly takes account of the seniority factor.

d. In most years, the position has been held by a university graduate in most branches.

e. Simple average of wages of workers with a fixed wage in all branches in Bogota.

Source: Company records and Fedesarrollo computations.

Table 7. *Average Real Monthly Salaries and Wages Paid to White-Collar Workers in Retail Trade, 1975–79*
(constant 1954 Colombian pesos)

Occupation	1975	1976	1977	1978	1979
Merchandise in general	248	260	255	282	306
Food and beverages	319	327	336	362	395
Clothing and footwear	265	294	279	293	310
Pharmaceutical products	247	236	241	279	300
Furniture and household appliances	437	456	483	500	470
Construction materials	341	421	409	391	386
Vehicles and spare parts	450	507	512	540	514
Fuels	297	359	388	396	397
Unclassified merchandise	377	363	349	348	352
Total	323	340	343	365	378

Note: Wages are deflated by the consumer price index: base 1954–55 = 100.
Source: DANE monthly statistical bulletins and Fedesarrollo computations.

Tables 6, 7, and 8 show, in general, that incomes in the services sector are much lower than those in trade. In both sectors, however, earnings are higher than the minimum wage.

For the manufacturing industry, data from institutional sources such as DANE, the Social Security Institute, and the Business Opinion Survey of Fedesarrollo, as well as from individual firms, were used to obtain as consistent a picture as possible of the trends in earnings (wages plus fringe benefits). In general, both white-collar and blue-collar workers in the manufacturing sector enjoyed an increase in real wages during the 1960s. The DANE Monthly Survey of Manufacturing shows gains of about 20 percent for both groups (see Figure 2). The annual survey shows the same trend, although, because of different methodologies and definitions, the order of magnitude is not the same.

During the 1970s, in contrast, white-collar and blue-collar workers suffered such a decrease in their real wages that by the middle of the decade they were earning less in real terms than they had ten years earlier. The decline is clear in the DANE monthly survey as well as in the annual survey and in the data of ISS and Fedesarrollo (see Table 9). Toward 1975–76, this trend began to be reversed and increases were observed in salaries and wages, although the level of the early 1960s was not regained until the end of the 1970s. Even in 1979, however, industrial wages had a lower purchasing power than at the beginning of the 1970s.

The DANE annual survey, which covers both wages and fringe benefits, shows that fringe benefits contributed significantly to improving the situation of wage earners during a period when basic salaries and wages were declining in real terms.[12] While the salaries and wages of executives and technical personnel and of white-collar workers in the manufacturing industry rose by 16 percent between 1964 and 1970 and fell by 18 percent between 1970 and 1976, total income (wages plus fringe benefits) rose by 28 percent and fell by 9 percent in the respective periods. The situation is similar in the case of production workers and laborers: salaries and wages showed a gain of 12 percent between 1964 and 1970 and an equal reduction of 12 percent between 1970 and 1976, whereas total earnings rose by 25 percent in the first of those periods and fell by only 5 percent in the second. Consequently, the difference between total labor income and salaries and wages has been widening. Salaries and wages of executive and technical personnel and of white-collar workers accounted for 80 percent of total income in 1962, 71 percent in 1970, and 64 percent in 1976, whereas the percentages for blue-collar workers were 79 percent, 70 percent, and 64 percent, respectively, in the same years.

In summary, all the data confirm the sluggish growth of wages in the manufacturing industry during the 1970s. But certain distinctions need to be made. First, if fringe benefits are added to the basic wage, total earnings perform better (see Table 10). Second, even in manufacturing, the poorer, unskilled workers did better than the skilled workers (see Table 11). Third, wages and total earnings have increased faster in small enterprises than in large ones (see Tables 12 and 13). All this has meant a decrease in income differentials in industry and relative gains on the part of the poorer workers. Finally, wage dispersion from industry to industry has decreased, particularly at the expense of the highly paid petroleum workers.

The Urban Middle Class

The middle class is difficult to define. A sociological definition would encompass a quite heterogeneous category. In surveys conducted in Japan, for example, the majority of the population declares that it belongs to the middle class. In Colombia, even persons in the highest decile of the income distribution believe that they belong to the middle class. A strict economic definition of the middle class would include persons who have incomes close to the national average. Thus, common usage includes in the middle class population groups different from those that an economist might include in that category.

Table 8. *Average Real Monthly Wages Paid by Service Firms, 1965–78*
(constant 1954 Colombian pesos)

Year	Restaurant basic wage[a]	Laundry		Hotel in Bogota[d]		
		Basic wage[b]	Wage and benefits[c]	Laundry[e]	Housekeeping[e]	Average[f]
1965	—	177	211	—	—	—
1966	—	148	175	—	—	—
1967	—	144	169	—	—	—
1968	136	146	178	—	—	—
1969	130	156	184	—	—	—
1970	142	142	167	—	—	—
1971	147	147	169	—	—	—
1972	131	131	151	140	138	138
1973	119	119	135	123	130	129
1974	119	119	137	115	129	127
1975	117	120	136	114	124	123
1976	122	124	140	126	139	137
1977	109	125	137	118	133	130
1978	126	140	154	133	149	145

—Data not available.

Note: Wages are deflated by the blue-collar consumer price index for Bogota: base 1954–55 = 100.

a. Average wage of a sample of fifteen persons in a total population of twenty-five (waiters, cashiers, cooks, kitchen helpers, and so forth).

b. Average wage of the total population of twenty-four (drivers, pressers, launderers, spot removers, markers, counter personnel, and so on).

c. Includes vacations, family allowance, transportation allowance, bonuses, and severance pay.

d. The data correspond to the basic wage plus night and holiday bonuses; the conversion from daily to monthly wage is based on twenty-five working days per month.

			Hotel in Girardot[g]					Handling of liquids[i]	
Cleaner	Laundry worker	Maid	Waiter	Cook	Bellhop	Porter	Average[h]	Basic wage	Real income[j]
108	78	109	163	108	77	100	168	—	—
92	65	91	137	91	65	83	138	212	340
105	74	99	139	96	74	109	143	200	338
104	84	102	152	102	84	111	154	189	354
113	107	108	262	113	105	118	167	197	326
123	156	124	268	124	150	160	184	202	325
127	190	156	265	144	185	192	212	242	345
137	180	183	270	183	179	212	218	219	344
162	193	194	257	204	193	203	218	189	410
153	180	202	242	210	180	188	203	190	363
145	157	184	286	185	156	178	197	179	314
162	198	173	252	180	198	201	202	181	338
143	153	153	223	157	153	164	175	186	280
153	132	137	213	137	153	141	165	188	265

e. These data are based on the average of a sample observed over eight two-week periods.

f. Average wage in the laundry and housekeeping unit, weighted by the number of employees in each unit.

g. The data correspond to basic wages plus overtime for a single person who has performed the job.

h. Simple average of a sample of twenty-four persons.

i. Average for the population of a firm engaged in the treatment of liquids, with plants in Bogota, Cartagena, and Buenaventura.

j. Basic wage plus overtime, bonuses, and allowances.

Source: Records of firms surveyed.

Figure 2. *Trends in Wages Paid in Manufacturing Industry and in National per Capita Income, 1962–79*

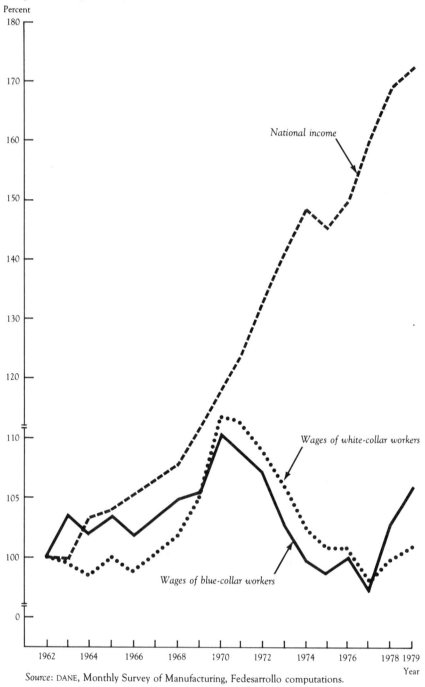

Source: DANE, Monthly Survey of Manufacturing, Fedesarrollo computations.

Table 9. *Indexes of Average Real Wages of Workers in the Manufacturing Industry, 1970–79*
(Base 1970 = 100)

Source	1970	1971	1972	1973	1974	1975	1976	1977	1978	1979
Annual survey										
Blue-collar	100	100	98	89	86	85	88	86	105	101
White-collar	100	103	98	89	87	81	82	79	89	87
Monthly sample										
Blue-collar	100	98	95	87	83	81	83	79	87	93
White-collar	100	99	94	89	84	82	82	77	80	82
Social Security Institute[a]										
Total	100	95	91	89	92	89	97	90	99	—
Business Opinion Survey[b]										
Blue-collar	—	—	100	92	87	90	85	84	94	93
White-collar	—	—	100	94	88	90	86	83	86	85

—Data not available.

a. Social Security wage services underestimate wage increases for the reasons given in note 8 of this chapter.

b. The Business Opinion Survey of Fedesarrollo was started in 1972, and the variations refer to the December/December averages (1972 = 100).

Source: DANE annual survey and monthly survey; Social Security Institute, *Informes Estadísticos*, various numbers; Fedesarrollo, *Encuesta de Opinon Empresarial*.

Table 10. *Percentage Change in Real Wages and Real Total Earnings of Blue-Collar and White-Collar Workers in the Manufacturing Industry, 1964–76*

Employment categories	1964–70	1970–76	1964–76
All white-collar workers' salaries	28	−18	5
Technical and managerial (White-collar) employees			
Salaries	16	−18	−4
Total earnings[a]	28	−9	17
Blue-collar workers			
Wages	12	−12	−1
Total earnings[a]	25	−5	19

a. Total earnings include wages plus fringe benefits.
Source: DANE.

In Colombia the middle class generally is considered to comprise white-collar workers and persons with a secondary education. This definition is quite consistent with economic reality. In fact, the 1977 DANE survey showed that the average income of a worker in Bogota was Col\$4,434 a month, very close to the average income for persons with a secondary education.[13] In other words, persons with a secondary education have incomes close to the average and can therefore be considered typically middle class. Because the distribution of income is not normal, however, the mean income is higher than the mode.[14] This suggests that the middle class defined in terms of education, or average income, probably would include people from the seventh to the ninth deciles of the income distribution.[15] In 1977, as shown in Table 3, the incomes of sales agents, production supervisors, and office workers approached the average income per worker. Thus, with a definition based on average income, those groups might be typical of the middle class.

But the characteristics of middle-class workers can be defined in greater detail on the basis of tabulations of a 1978 household survey. Table 14, which displays the distribution of income by occupation for males in Bogota, shows an average income of about Col\$10,000 per month. The average income in several occupations approximately equals the national average: teachers; accounting clerks, bank employees, and cashiers; business managers; and merchants. In other words, the middle class could include white-collar workers, merchants, and teachers.[16] Some blue-collar occupations, however, also account for substantial proportions of the labor force in the seventh to ninth deciles, which we have defined as the middle class.

Table 11. *Percentage Change in Real Remuneration of Labor by Branch of Economic Activity, 1962–79*

Branch of activity	1962–69	1970–79
Manufacturing industry blue-collar workers	12.0	−6.9
Industries in which unskilled workers are predominant[a]		
Food (20)	22.2	−0.4
Tobacco (22)	−18.0	−23.8
Footwear and clothing (24)	1.1	9.9
Wood industry (25)	0.5	−6.0
Wooden furniture (26)	0.4	−11.0
Leather and leather products (29)	20.5	−8.1
Metal products except machinery (35)	5.5	−1.2
Average[a]	9.5	0.5
Industries in which skilled workers are predominant[a]		
Petroleum products (32)	−0.8	−26.2
Beverages (21)	0.6	−8.0
Textiles (23)	23.1	−12.9
Paper and paper products (27)	33.2	6.2
Rubber products (30)	27.1	−0.6
Basic metals (34)	37.8	−25.8
Average[a]	29.8	−11.0
Manufacturing industry white-collar workers	10.0	−18.3
Total construction[b]	4.9	13.0
Master	0.2	−1.6
Journeyman	7.1	17.6
Helper	7.9	17.0
Financial sector		
Professional	18.1	−20.6
Nonprofessional (with 15 years of experience)	43.9	−7.0
Nonprofessional (with 10 years of experience)	—	40.1
Government sector		
Professional (Ministry of Finance)	−21.6	−32.9
Executive	—	−10.6
Primary school teacher	—	2.7
Secondary school teacher	—	−5.4
Manager of electrification plant	—	−37.4
Head of personnel	—	−12.4
Lineman	—	10.0
National government white-collar workers	1.0	—
Departmental government white-collar workers	1.0	—
Municipal white-collar workers	7.0	—

—Data not available.

a. Weighted average based on participation in employment. Based on DANE manufacturing survey, 1968.

b. 1962–70: Data from small construction firm; 1972–79: DANE, Bogota. The periods are different from those covered in the case of manufacturing.

Source: DANE, annual survey, and records of firms.

Table 12. *Average Real Monthly Salaries and Wages in the Manufacturing Industry by the Number of Persons Employed in the Enterprise, 1963–76*
(constant 1954 Colombian pesos)

Number employed	1963	1964	1965	1966	1967	1968	1969	1970	1971	1972	1973	1974	1975	1976
Fewer than 5	119	109	106	109	140	109	144	151	168	151	139	147	161	166
5–9	136	122	120	116	139	132	158	158	157	177	164	164	153	155
10–14	168	153	150	141	174	166	175	180	176	173	158	157	160	163
15–19	216	203	209	187	193	199	192	191	196	184	169	167	162	167
20–24	230	215	218	209	211	207	207	197	193	203	176	177	173	174
25–49	247	232	246	232	234	234	222	230	227	216	197	191	189	194
50–74	283	277	276	257	264	263	267	265	262	245	224	219	214	214
75–99	291	273	293	284	305	296	274	297	293	292	253	252	232	251
100–199	340	336	342	327	333	338	334	352	339	316	294	278	265	281
200 and more	360	365	379	372	395	393	386	427	433	420	377	362	356	364

Note: The wage and salary figures are deflated by the national consumer price index: base 1954–55 = 100.

Source: DANE, Annual Survey of Manufacturing, and Fedesarrollo computations.

Table 13. *Average Real Monthly Salaries, Wages, and Employee Benefits in the Manufacturing Industry by the Number of Persons Employed in the Enterprise, 1963–76*
(constant 1954 Colombian pesos)

Number employed	1963	1964	1965	1966	1967	1968	1969	1970	1971	1972	1973	1974	1975	1976
Fewer than 5	127	117	113	120	160	118	161	170	191	174	166	170	203	216
5–9	150	135	133	128	155	149	184	182	183	211	194	200	188	199
10–14	190	174	170	162	201	192	208	214	212	208	191	194	202	212
15–19	249	236	246	220	228	236	233	234	238	226	210	209	205	220
20–24	266	254	258	246	253	249	257	243	239	253	218	223	224	230
25–49	293	279	295	282	290	287	283	288	287	276	250	247	248	265
50–74	346	343	346	321	332	330	356	343	338	322	294	194	295	303
75–99	358	343	362	259	393	386	369	382	389	391	346	345	320	358
100–199	420	429	436	434	451	455	461	476	469	439	412	390	388	420
200 and more	490	493	518	515	561	562	582	647	629	633	579	566	572	594

Note: The figures used here are deflated by the national consumer price index: base 1954–55 = 100.
Source: DANE, Annual Survey of Manufacturing, and Fedesarrollo computations.

Table 14. *Distribution of Income by Occupation for Males in Bogota, 1978*
(income in 1978, Colombian pesos a month)

Occupation	Fourth decile	Fifth decile	Sixth decile	Seventh decile	Eighth decile	Ninth decile	Tenth decile	Total
Architects and engineers								
Row percentage		0	1.53	0	6.60	21.98	60.82	100
Column percentage	0	0	0.39	0	1.26	4.69	10.52	2.07
Average labor income	—	—	0	—	11,230	23,596	32,146	25,517
Average other income	—	—	0	—	0	2,629	4,837	3,518
Medical doctors and dentists								
Row percentage	0	0	5.10	1.47	6.20	38.28	47.22	100
Column percentage	0	0	1.32	0.43	1.20	8.52	8.52	2.79
Average labor income	—	—	4,008	—	13,713	20,056	35,202	25,451
Average other income	—	—	—	—	0	96	2,320	1,133
Accountants								
Row percentage	12.60	0	0	5.09	18.05	11.47	52.79	100
Column percentage	4.02	0	0	1.41	3.50	2.44	9.09	2.66
Average labor income	9,052	—	—	11,477	12,157	13,303	34,149	23,473
Average other income	2,565	—	—	0	1,606	4,249	4,237	3,368
Jurists								
Row percentage	1.87	0	0	2.25	4.62	19.10	70.11	100
Column percentage	0.49	0	0	0.51	0.73	3.32	9.90	2.18
Average labor income	8,000	—	—	14,300	8,811	16,550	39,453	31,767
Average other income	0	—	—	0	0	0	2,277	1,596
Teachers								
Row percentage	6.02	6.43	8.93	7.21	14.36	23.41	26.40	100
Column percentage	2.67	2.60	3.06	2.78	3.37	6.90	8.32	3.69
Average labor income	5,139	5,501	6,991	9,569	8,103	13,655	23,364	12,717
Average other income	79	387	0	0	973	1,166	1,899	959

Managers and executives								
Row percentage	1.58	0	7.95	0.77	10.56	20.63	55.98	100
Column percentage	1.25	0	4.85	0.53	5.07	10.85	23.88	6.59
Average labor income	2,517	—	10,710	6,750	12,967	17,218	34,939	25,423
Average other income	2,676	—	0	0	2,444	1,468	4,005	2,845
Bookkeepers, bank employees, cashiers, and others								
Row percentage	6.40	7.61	11.34	13.23	16.70	21.97	17.74	100
Column percentage	5.67	6.13	7.76	10.21	8.99	12.95	8.48	7.38
Average labor income	6,333	4,818	6,771	6,768	7,080	8,156	11,918	7,701
Average other income	0	0	332	231	513	410	1,159	450
Mailmen and messengers								
Row percentage	14.65	21.36	10.26	18.80	16.69	4.39	1.12	100
Column percentage	4.67	6.22	2.53	5.22	3.23	0.93	0.19	2.66
Average labor income	5,392	2,523	3,247	3,029	3,120	3,193	2,915	3,399
Average other income	0	0	0	303	0	0	0	57
Managers in the commercial sector								
Row percentage	10.93	6.70	11.41	11.14	20.15	32.91	3.48	100
Column percentage	1.54	0.86	1.24	1.37	1.73	3.09	0.26	1.17
Average labor income	3,097	8,667	5,581	5,946	14,560	17,581	29,167	12,021
Average other income	0	0	0	0	0	895	0	294
Merchants and shop owners								
Row percentage	8.60	7.09	8.12	7.77	12.95	15.20	11.77	100
Column percentage	12.97	9.77	9.46	10.20	11.86	15.25	9.58	12.37
Average labor income	3,649	5,130	5,991	7,263	9,262	14,535	39,136	10,380
Average other income	841	552	175	1,054	1,621	337	1,937	722
Salesmen and trade employees								
Row percentage	8.69	11.26	15.04	9.88	11.07	8.96	7.05	100
Column percentage	14.87	17.59	19.58	14.71	11.51	10.20	6.51	14.26
Average labor income	3,635	4,104	4,132	5,779	8,337	8,870	23,814	6,085
Average other income	185	362	162	436	291	—	2,873	374

(Table continues on the following page)

Table 14 (continued)

Occupation	Fourth decile	Fifth decile	Sixth decile	Seventh decile	Eighth decile	Ninth decile	Tenth decile	Total
Cooks, waiters, and others								
Row percentage	16.55	6.82	19.14	20.16	7.81	0	0	100
Column percentage	2.93	1.10	2.62	3.11	0.84	0	0	1.47
Average labor income	3,975	4,092	4,583	5,281	3,883	—	—	4,374
Average other income	0	1,291	0	0	0	—	—	88
Security guards and night watchmen								
Row percentage	9.92	10.66	10.33	8.35	12.47	5.35	0.58	100
Column percentage	8.92	8.75	7.21	6.55	6.82	3.20	0.28	7.50
Average labor income	3,770	5,464	4,648	5,928	4,920	3,792	75,650	4,682
Average other income	244	913	832	250	298	3,175	0	466
Farmers and cattle ranchers								
Row percentage	0	0	8.38	0	16.65	15.39	25.28	100
Column percentage	0	0	1.00	0	1.56	1.58	2.10	1.28
Average labor income	—	—	6,280	—	17,375	17,549	48,648	18,537
Average other income	—	—	0	—	0	1,423	8,085	2,454
Agricultural workers								
Row percentage	12.42	0	35.93	8.47	0	11.29	0	100
Column percentage	0.54	0	1.20	0.32	0	0.33	0	0.36
Average labor income	3,201	—	5,073	4,500	—	3,500	—	3,772
Average other income	0	—	0	0	—	0	—	0
Foremen, supervisors, and overseers								
Row percentage	2.80	8.98	19.89	22.56	27.56	13.17	0	100
Column percentage	0.56	1.64	3.07	3.92	3.34	1.75	0	1.66
Average labor income	5,810	6,369	7,946	7,130	7,665	16,384	—	8,408
Average other income	0	0	0	0	0	629	—	83
Food industry workers								
Row percentage	11.99	14.87	4.55	13.24	12.79	7.04	0	100
Column percentage	3.79	4.29	1.11	3.65	2.46	1.48	0	2.63

Average labor income	3,592	4,028	5,209	4,742	7,830	5,927	—	4,422
Average other income	79	0	0	0	0	0	—	10
Tailors, dressmakers, upholsterers, and others								
Row percentage	5.94	25.34	18.19	4.78	11.45	4.47	0	100
Column percentage	2.09	8.15	4.95	1.47	2.45	1.05	0	2.94
Average labor income	3,168	3,633	5,948	5,587	5,024	5,004	—	4,060
Average other income	0	76	0	0	0	0	—	20
Cabinetmakers and woodworking machine operators								
Row percentage	8.02	19.57	15.62	9.58	19.34	0	0	100
Column percentage	3.18	4.86	3.29	2.27	3.20	0	0	2.27
Average labor income	5,490	2,695	3,385	6,305	5,594	—	—	4,077
Average other income	280	256	320	0	22	—	—	168
Metalworkers								
Row percentage	8.55	9.32	11.06	13.01	18.01	9.10	4.16	100
Column percentage	5.34	5.32	5.33	7.08	6.84	3.78	1.40	5.20
Average labor income	3,343	3,190	4,570	6,028	5,650	7,286	15,417	5,074
Average other income	0	0	486	68	0	334	0	109
Machinery fitters, machine assemblers and installers, precision instrument mechanics, and watchmakers								
Row percentage	13.09	12.41	10.30	16.44	13.96	8.03	4.44	100
Column percentage	14.71	12.73	8.94	16.10	9.54	6.00	2.70	9.37
Average labor income	4,203	4,529	5,535	4,802	7,193	10,782	13,048	5,606
Average other income	37	0	273	76	3,865	0	1,790	696
Electrical workers and the like								
Row percentage	18.04	16.16	20.84	7.61	17.47	3.55	0	100
Column percentage	7.74	7.12	6.91	2.84	4.55	1.01	0	3.58
Average labor income	3,762	5,099	6,685	8,241	5,778	6,381	—	5,324
Average other income	0	137	324	687	845	569	—	313

(Table continues on the following page)

Table 14 (continued)

Occupation	Fourth decile	Fifth decile	Sixth decile	Seventh decile	Eighth decile	Ninth decile	Tenth decile	Total
Plumbers, welders, and metal and structural metal preparers and installers								
Row percentage	8.26	8.41	13.61	16.47	23.84	2.78	1.32	100
Column percentage	3.07	2.85	3.90	5.33	5.38	0.69	0.26	3.10
Average labor income	3,576	5,451	6,548	4,475	5,254	6,503	10,000	4,740
Average other income	0	0	0	0	0	982	5,000	93
Total								
Row percentage	8.33	9.13	10.79	9.57	13.71	12.52	15.44	100
Column percentage[a]	100	100	100	100	100	100	100	100
Average labor income	4,265	4,393	5,593	5,976	7,854	13,118	31,434	10,072
Average other income	312	250	218	264	918	767	3,101	314

—Data not available.

a. The column figures don't add up to 100 because certain occupations are not included in the table. For example, stonecutters and carvers were not included because they were represented only in the second decile.

Source: DANE, 1978 household survey.

42

These include a proportion of skilled workers, such as plumbers; welders; metalworkers; fabricators and assemblers of metal structures; adjusters, assemblers, and installers of precision machinery and instruments; watchmakers; mechanics; overseers, supervisors, and foremen; and even workers in the food industry. In short, the middle class includes some skilled industrial workers.

In addition, these three deciles also include a proportion of workers who in general would be assumed to be part of the upper-middle class. Examples are certain doctors, accountants, directors or executive personnel, and farmers and stockmen residing in Bogota.

In summary, if the middle class is defined as the group of workers with incomes close to the urban average, it would include those falling between the seventh and ninth deciles of the family income distribution. The typical members of this group are white-collar workers, merchants, and teachers, but the group also includes large numbers of skilled workers, middle-level managers, and some professionals. Most professionals are, of course, in the highest decile of the distribution and are part of the upper class, even if they do not so consider themselves. As Table 14 shows, 61 percent of the architects and 70 percent of the lawyers are in the highest decile of the distribution.

The decline in the real incomes of white-collar workers in the manufacturing industry was noted earlier. Apparently, the income of blue-collar workers and other unskilled persons rose faster than the incomes of white-collar workers during the latter part of the decade.

Table 11 divides the industrial sector into groupings of skilled and unskilled industrial workers to permit an analysis of trends in the incomes of those skilled workers who, on the basis of household survey data, may be part of the middle class. The clothing, food, and wood industries are characterized by high proportions of unskilled labor. The opposite is true of the paper, petroleum products, and basic metals industries. The real incomes of the two groups behaved differently. In the 1960s, the real incomes of the skilled groups increased more than those of the unskilled. During this period, there was also a high return on education, as a number of studies on investment in human capital show.

During the 1970s, the returns to education decreased along with the real incomes of skilled workers and white-collar personnel.[17] From 1970 to 1979, the real incomes of blue-collar workers in industries requiring a high skill level fell by 11 percent, not much less than the 18 percent decrease observed for white-collar workers in industry.

In short, the 1960s were good for the middle class and the 1970s were not. For the period as a whole, the lower segments of the middle class

Table 15. *Average Real Monthly Wages in Government Agencies, 1960–79*
(constant 1954 Colombian pesos)

| Year | Ministry of Finance | | | | District office Public Works Dept. (unskilled) | |
	Professional[a]	Messenger[a]	Cleaner[a]	Average for a department[b]	Retired[c]	Active[d]
1960	1,545	184	124	—	—	—
1961	1,613	234	175	—	—	—
1962	1,531	229	171	—	—	—
1963	1,271	173	130	—	—	—
1964	1,663	154	154	—	—	—
1965	1,561	220	185	—	—	—
1966	1,445	267	225	—	—	—
1967	1,318	247	208	—	—	—
1968	1,329	254	230	656	—	—
1969	1,230	230	209	610	—	—
1970	1,211	227	206	583	—	—
1971	1,159	218	198	557	207	187
1972	1,278	200	182	647	209	192
1973	1,110	171	155	629	199	189
1974	1,045	205	169	553	195	180
1975	1,021	195	161	539	187	178
1976	898	173	143	521	202	192
1977	852	205	163	551	191	182
1978	825	221	185	575	202	189
1979	813	227	210	527	196	185

—Data not available.

Note: The wage figures are deflated by the consumer price index for blue-collar and white-collar workers in Bogota and Medellin as applicable. Base: 1954–55 = 100.

a. Basic wage. *Source:* Up to 1967, Miguel Urrutia and Mario Arrubla, *Compendio de Estadisticas Historicas de Colombia* (Bogota: Universidad Nacional, 1970). For 1968–79, records of the Ministry of Finance.

b. Simple average of basic wages of all Direccion General de Presupuesto employees, excluding the director.

c. Basic wage in August taken from budget for the year. Average for thirty-one persons. Conversion factor daily to monthly: twenty-five.

d. Basic wage in August, taken from budget for forty persons. Daily converted to monthly.

		Boyaca electricity company					
		Manager		Head of personnel		Lineman	
Teachers in Antioquia[e]							
Primary[f]	Secondary[f]	Salary[g]	Income[h]	Salary[i]	Income[h]	Salary[i]	Income[h]
—	—	—	—	—	—	—	—
—	—	1,792	—	508	—	—	—
—	—	2,268	—	567	—	—	—
—	—	—	—	530	—	—	—
—	—	2,462	—	685	—	—	—
—	—	2,363	—	788	—	—	—
—	—	1,990	—	680	—	—	—
—	—	2,006	—	645	—	—	—
383	504	2,338	2,481	700	930	392	420
364	478	2,398	2,712	683	1,028	364	452
365	496	2,616	2,903	785	1,065	343	424
371	518	2,413	3,070	—	—	345	431
360	513	2,183	—	713	885	358	439
322	490	2,186	2,729	779	1,039	346	404
397	498	2,480	2,733	687	876	298	383
357	605	2,396	2,892	603	767	334	372
309	530	2,049	2,517	—	—	354	374
293	498	1,633	2,009	702	—	277	325
330	498	1,669	2,011	708	788	289	358
375	470	1,637	—	688	—	309	338

e. Total population taken into account. Source: Records of Fondo Educativo Regional, Antioquia.

f. Monthly average per teacher, including bonuses.

g. Including basic wage, plus cost-of-living and entertainment allowances. The figure shown is the statutory salary for that job.

h. Including overtime and allowances. Excluding the following payments: retirement compensation and bonuses, living allowance, medical care, dental services, opthalmological services, payment of electricity charges, and so forth.

i. Including basic wage plus cost-of-living allowance. The data reflect the actual earnings of a person holding that job.

Source: Records of the government agencies.

enjoyed greater gains than the upper segments, if one considers that white-collar workers have higher incomes than skilled workers.

Data on the financial sector confirm this conclusion. The personnel of one bank studied had smaller income gains than skilled industrial workers, particularly during the 1970s. Within that bank, personnel below the professional level also enjoyed relatively larger wage increases than more skilled individuals.

Table 15 presents some data on the monthly wages in the public sector. Although professionals working in the Ministry of Finance suffered a clear decline in salaries, unskilled personnel in the same ministry saw some improvement in their income. During the 1970s, the real incomes of messengers, cleaning staff, and blue-collar workers in the public works department in the federal district remained constant. In general, that part of the middle class comprising government white-collar workers lost out in relative terms; the loss was much more pronounced for skilled personnel.

Wage surveys conducted in industries by consulting firms show that the upper-middle class also did not have large real wage gains. Although there are problems in trying to compare the data over time, these series confirm the decline in the relative position of the middle class. Table 16 shows a reduction in the real incomes of white-collar workers and supervisors in industry, particularly during the 1970s. Table 17 indicates a general stagnation in the wages of higher-level white-collar workers in 1977–79, a period when the wages of agricultural daily workers and the incomes of unskilled workers (including the unskilled white-collar workers in Table 17) were rising. Table 18, based on a different source, shows the same trends.

Little information is available on the incomes of the upper class. Nonetheless, a number of indicators suggest that the earnings of this group rose rapidly during the 1970s. One such indicator is the rapid expansion of the supply of luxury housing and the sharp rise in real prices for such housing. Increases in automobile sales, shown in Table 19, also seem to reflect the rising incomes of the highest decile of the distribution. Since the income of the middle class did not rise during the decade, it may be assumed that the majority of the automobile purchases were made by the upper class.[18] The number of automobiles per 100 households in the wealthiest sector of Bogota rose by 8 percent between 1972 and 1978.[19] In the second wealthiest area, the ownership of automobiles per 100 families decreased. The data on changes in automobile ownership, therefore, confirm the rapid rise in the incomes of the wealthiest families and the stagnation or decrease in the incomes of the middle class. In some lower-

Table 16. *Trends in the Monthly Remuneration of Selected Executive, Production, and Shop Personnel, 1961–79*
(constant 1954 Colombian pesos)

Occupation	July 1961 [a]	November 1962 [b]	July 1968 [c]	First half 1972 [d]	Second half 1976 [e]	March 1979 [f]
Beginning engineer	1,065	1,140	1,077	—	—	—
Engineer (with two years' experience)	1,432	1,500	1,474	—	—	—
Head of production[g]	2,569	1,996	2,098	2,803	2,144	2,196
Head of engineering[h]	2,459	2,236	2,994	3,057	2,087	1,867
Head of industrial relations	1,866	—	2,428	3,134	2,706	2,787
Head of industrial relations (plant)	—	—	—	1,703	1,642	1,622
Production manager	—	—	—	2,533	2,162	2,062
Financial manager	—	—	—	3,767	3,541	3,220
Head of accounting section	—	—	—	1,143	964	865
Production supervisor[i]	659	—	646	1,228	1,091	926
Maintenance shop supervisor[j]	664	769	728	1,209	785	546

—Data not available.

Note: The figures are deflated by the consumer price index for white-collar workers: base 1954–55 = 100. The price index for Cali was used for the 1961, 1962, 1968 data; for the other years, the national consumer price index was used for the month of the survey, or the average for the year or six-month period, as appropriate.

a. Eleven firms surveyed.
b. Seven firms surveyed.
c. Eight firms surveyed.
d. Thirty-two firms surveyed.
e. Sixty-six firms surveyed.
f. Fifty-eight firms surveyed.
g. From 1972, same as head of production department.
h. From 1972, same as head of plant engineering and subsequently head of project engineering.
i. In 1972, same as general production supervisor and in 1976–79 same as production supervisor.
j. Beginning in 1972, same as maintenance supervisor.

Source: Asesorías y Servicios Industriales. Information for years before 1972 is based on a summary of salary and wage surveys made in 1961, 1965, and 1968 for firms interested in the preparation of salary scales in the Cali area. From 1972 onward, the results correspond to a semiannual survey of salaries and benefits.

Table 17. *Average Monthly Salaries for Selected Executive and Office Positions, 1977 and 1979*
(Colombian pesos)

Position	1977[a]		1979[b]	
	Current prices	Constant prices[c]	Current prices	Constant prices[c]
Accounting supervisor				
National market average	20,395	1,283	—	—
Food and beverages	25,567	1,608	27,478	1,173
Textiles and apparel	20,911	1,315	26,891	1,148
Metalworking	19,946	1,254	27,982	1,195
Pharmaceuticals and chemicals	24,675	1,552	32,550	1,390
Other manufacturers	17,834	1,122	24,475	1,173
Manufacturing	20,451	1,286	28,105	1,200
Marketing chains	20,250	1,273	—	—
Banks and financial institutions	19,833	1,247	—	—
General accounting assistant				
National market average	5,444	342	—	—
Food and beverages	5,701	358	9,791	418
Textiles and apparel	5,723	359	8,277	353
Metalworking	5,351	336	8,407	359
Pharmaceuticals and chemicals	6,855	431	9,810	419
Other manufactures	6,456	406	10,429	445
Manufacturing	6,021	379	9,345	399
Marketing chains	5,019	316	—	—
Banks and financial institutions	4,408	277	—	—
General cashier				
National market average	6,875	432	—	—
Food and beverages	8,458	532	13,871	592
Textiles and apparel	8,687	546	11,673	499
Metalworking	9,331	587	12,831	548
Pharmaceuticals and chemicals	8,401	528	11,941	510
Other manufactures	8,807	554	11,365	485
Manufacturing	9,019	567	12,409	530
Marketing chains	10,355	651	—	—
Banks and financial institutions	5,227	329	—	—
Payroll officer				
National market average	7,464	469	—	—
Food and beverages	7,378	465	12,246	523
Textiles and apparel	7,868	495	11,268	481
Metalworking	7,056	444	10,829	462
Pharmaceuticals and chemicals	7,226	454	12,335	527
Other manufactures	8,063	507	13,968	596
Manufacturing	7,592	477	12,228	522
Marketing chains	8,049	506	—	—
Banks and financial institutions	6,493	408	—	—

Position	1977[a]		1979[b]	
	Current prices	Constant prices[c]	Current prices	Constant prices[c]
Receptionist				
National market average	3,999	251	—	—
Food and beverages	4,419	278	6,722	287
Textiles and apparel	4,049	255	6,059	259
Metalworking	4,054	255	5,985	255
Pharmaceuticals and chemicals	4,479	282	6,443	275
Other manufactures	4,559	283	7,307	312
Manufacturing	4,330	272	6,553	280
Marketing chains	3,372	212	—	—
Banks and financial institutions	3,483	219	—	—
Internal messenger				
National market average	2,647	166	—	—
Food and beverages	3,574	225	6,510	278
Textiles and apparel	3,250	204	5,056	216
Metalworking	2,733	172	5,039	215
Pharmaceuticals and chemicals	3,337	210	5,108	218
Other manufactures	3,392	213	5,515	235
Manufacturing	3,281	206	5,377	230
Marketing chains	2,390	150	—	—
Banks and other institutions	2,276	143	—	—
Cleaning worker				
National market average	2,526	159	—	—
Food and beverages	3,408	214	5,366	229
Textiles and apparel	2,849	179	4,959	212
Metalworking	2,915	183	5,479	234
Pharmaceuticals and chemicals	2,965	186	5,050	216
Other manufactures	3,463	218	5,484	234
Manufacturing	3,113	196	5,252	224
Marketing chains	2,024	127	—	—
Banks and financial institutions	2,495	157	—	—

a. Results of a national salary survey conducted in 122 firms located in four departments. Information as of May 31, 1977.

b. Results of a national salary survey conducted in 132 firms located in five departments. Information for the first six months of 1979.

c. Deflated by the national consumer price index for white-collar workers: base 1954–55 = 100.

Source: Specialized consulting firm.

Table 18. *Average Real Monthly Remuneration to Labor in Selected Executive and Office Positions, 1977 and 1979*
(constant 1954 Colombian pesos)

Position	1977 [a]		1979 [b]	
	Basic wage [c]	Total remuneration [d]	Basic wage [c]	Total remuneration [d]
Executive positions [e]				
Financial director	3,696	4,110	3,890	4,138
Plant manager	3,482	3,870	3,702	3,872
Production manager	2,092	2,342	2,373	2,526
General and cost accountant	1,654	1,828	1,707	1,823
Office positions				
Bilingual executive secretary, management	942	1,047	1,010	1,087
Spanish-speaking secretary, Class I	580	649	538	580
Stenographer-typist	396	445	406	439
Receptionist	358	396	342	371
Messenger	247	276	296	320

Note: Figures are deflated by the national consumer price index for white-collar workers: base 1954–55 = 100.

a. The survey covered twenty companies, of which twelve operate in the medical products market and the remaining eight in mass consumption products. At the management and administration levels, fifty-two positions were surveyed. The twenty companies had over 7,800 employees, of whom 35 percent were members of trade unions. The survey was conducted in 1976 on salaries and extra-legal benefits that would be in effect in 1977.

b. In 1979, eighteen companies were included. The survey was conducted in May 1979, and the results were projected through December.

c. Based on the average of thirteen months' basic wages, including the legal bonus for services.

d. Including the basic wage plus extra-legal benefits.

e. In 1979, a large percentage of those holding executive positions had company cars (especially the financial director, plant manager, and marketing manager). In some cases, moreover, club memberships were paid for the employee, together with a percentage of the basic monthly wage as "permanent allowances." (The percentage ranged from a low of 10 percent to a high of 50 percent.)

Source: Private consulting firm.

Table 19. *Number of Private Automobiles Sold in Colombia, 1970–80*

	1970	1971[a]	1972	1973	1974	1975	1976	1977	1978	1979	1980[b]
Total	4,972	11,586	16,612	22,304	28,954	25,047	24,684	28,752	35,355	32,651	19,746
Domestic	3,851	10,703	15,668	20,413	27,093	23,238	23,347	27,275	33,342	30,670	16,177
Imported	1,121	803	944	1,819	1,861	1,809	1,337	1,477	2,013	1,981	3,569
Percentage of total imported	22.5	6.9	5.7	8.2	6.4	7.2	5.4	5.1	5.7	6.1	18.1
Mid-size automobiles											
Domestic[c]	355	1,826	5,692	8,620	9,858	8,090	9,979	12,183	16,195	13,749	10,439
Imported[d]	350	228	294	974	684	1,016	600	612	474	426	2,248
Large-size automobiles											
Domestic											
Imported[e]		75	104	228	218	186	209	150	326	309	169
Luxury automobiles											
Domestic[f]	1,364	2,467	1,703	1,324	1,790	1,987	1,830	2,127	2,834	2,403	1,080
Imported[g]	725	556	526	673	926	610	522	679	1,163	1,236	1,152

a. Renault began production in 1971.
b. Data for the first six months.
c. Dodge 1800, Renault 12.
d. Alpine, Fiat 125.
e. Ford, Datsun, BMW.
f. Dart, Coronado, Ford. There are no large-size automobiles produced domestically.
g. Mercedes, BMW.
Source: Compania Colombia Automotriz.

middle-class and middle-middle-class sectors of the city, ownership of automobiles increased. This supports the other evidence presented in this chapter, which suggests that the income differential within the middle class may have been reduced during the decade. The next chapter, which analyzes the income trends of the upper class and the lower class in Cali, also confirms these impressions about the incomes of the highest decile of the distribution.

Conclusion

All of the information compiled on incomes by occupational categories points to the conclusion that the middle class lost part of its share of national income during the 1970s. It is even possible that the real incomes of this group declined. Nonetheless, to be certain of this latter conclusion, one would have to analyze the participation of members of middle-class families in the labor force. The increased participation of females may have permitted families to maintain their standards of living during the period. While the gap between the income of poor agricultural workers and small farmers, and other workers probably decreased, among urban workers the poor and the unskilled did better than the skilled and those employed in the formal sector.

Notes to Chapter 2

1. Miguel Urrutia and Albert Berry, *La Distribucion del Ingreso en Colombia* (Medellin: Editorial la Carreta, 1975), tables 1 and 2 of chapter 1.

2. W. Arthur Lewis, "Development with Unlimited Supplies of Labour," *The Manchester School*, vol. 27, no. 2 (1954), pp. 139–92.

3. Kazuchi Ohkawa and Gustav Ranis, "On Phasing" (Paper presented at the Conference on Japan's Historical Development Experience and Contemporary Developing Countries, Tokyo, 1978; processed).

4. John C. H. Fei and Gustav Ranis, for example, have concluded this from their studies of the Republic of Korea and Taiwan. The theory is summarized in Ohkawa and Ranis, "On Phasing."

5. Although it would be better to compare growth in wages with growth in income per worker, there are no data on the economically active population for the noncensus years, and, given the instability of labor force participation rates, it was felt unwise to estimate those figures. Nevertheless, it is clear that between 1950 and 1970, population grew faster than the labor force. In that case, average income per employed worker grew faster than the agricultural wage in that period and, therefore, agricultural workers probably saw their relative income position deteriorate. In contrast, between 1965 and 1980, the labor force grew more rapidly than population, so the rate of growth per employed worker was lower than the 3.67 percent growth in per capita income (see the income figure at the bottom of column 4 in Table 2). It is, therefore, very clear that rural laborers improved their relative position in the period 1965–79 (while population grew 52 percent during

1965–80, the labor force grew 64 percent). The 1965 figure comes from International Labour Office (ILO), *Labour Force Estimates and Projections 1950–2000* (Geneva, 1977), p. 34. The 1980 figures are from *La Economica Colombiana en la Decada de los Ochenta* (Bogota: Fedesarrollo, 1979), p. 43 and p. 70.

6. Municipal wages are weighed by the population figures of each municipality, once the population of the major city in the district is subtracted. The average wage of populous municipalities has, therefore, a larger weight in the departmental average.

7. If female wages are considered in the calculation of the most frequent wage by municipality, the new methodology would lower the wage level. If the distribution of municipal wages by department is skewed and dispersion is large, average wages will be higher than most frequent wages. This would mean that the second methodology may produce higher wage levels.

8. The agricultural wage series published by the Social Security Institute was analyzed and discarded. A small proportion of employers in the rural sector affiliate their workers to ICSS (Instituto Colombiano de Seguros Sociales), because ICSS has few clinics in the rural sector. An exception might be Valle, where the big sugar plantations have been traditionally affiliated and where ICSS has clinics in many of Valle's towns. The employers originally affiliated to ICSS were the high-wage, large-scale, and capital-intensive enterprises. As ICSS services penetrated into the countryside, smaller and lower-wage employers joined, such as the companies producing flowers for export, which usually employ women at the minimum wage. Because of the entrance in the 1970s of smaller firms into the ICSS network, the social security wage data would appear to have a serious bias toward underestimating wage trends.

9. Helena Jaramillo, "Determinants of Income Differentials after Migration" (New Haven: Yale University, 1978; processed); and Rakesh Mohan, *The People of Bogota: Who They Are, What They Earn, Where They Live*, World Bank Staff Working Paper no. 390 (Washington, D.C., 1980).

10. Urrutia and Berry, *La Distribucion*.

11. This is not surprising when it is considered that agroindustry has pushed up agricultural wages in the department of Valle. In 1977, for example, Gomez-Angel discovered that in the squatter district of Cali the percentage of poor families who have electrical appliances was about the same as that for 479 families on a sugar plantation in the rural area of Valle. This suggests similar income levels. See Jairo, Gomez-Angel, "Traditional and Emerging Patterns in the Social Organization of a Large Estate in the Cauca Valley" (Ph.D. dissertation, Louisiana State University, August 1979).

12. The DANE annual survey defines salaries and wages as the fixed or ordinary remuneration that the worker received during the month in return for services rendered before deduction of items withheld at the source, such as social security, union dues, and the like. Employee fringe benefits comprise compulsory or voluntary payments other than salaries and wages made by employers to their employees.

13. Mohan, *The People of Bogota*. In July 1983, one U.S. dollar was roughly equal to 80 Colombian pesos (Col$).

14. Most income distributions are skewed, as opposed to normal, because there are many more people in the lower incomes than in the higher. This means that the most frequent income (mode) is in the low-income ranges, but the few high-income earners increase the average so that it is usually quite a bit higher than the modal income.

15. The DANE household survey for December 1978 found that average per capita income in Bogota was Col$7,010 a month, while the average income of the eighth decile of the distribution of per capita income per household was Col$6,851 a month.

16. The data on salaries and wages of white-collar workers in industry would also place them in these intervals of the distribution.

17. See François Bourguignon, "Probleza y Dualismo en el Sector Urbano de las Economias en Desarrollo: El Caso de Colombia," *Desarrollo y Sociedad* (January 1979), and Bernardo Kugler, Alvaro Reyes, and Maria Isabel de Gomez, *Educacion y Mercado de Trabajo Urbano en Colombia:*

Una Comparacion entre Sectores Moderno y no Moderno, monograph 10 (Bogota: Corporacion Centro Regional de Poblacion, 1979).

18. According to Pachon, 73 percent of the households in the highest decile had an automobile in 1978, and 22 percent of those families had two or more cars. Only 40 percent of the families in the ninth decile and 20 percent in the eighth decile had an automobile. See Alvaro Pachon, "Automobile Ownership in Bogota and Cali" (The World Bank City Study Workshop, Bogota, February 13, 1980; processed).

19. Ibid., tables 1–6 and 201. The average monthly income in this section of Bogota in 1978 was Col$31,030 per family, whereas the city average was Col$13,150.

3

Changes in Real Income of a Set of Rich and Poor Families in Cali

WAGE SERIES SHOW AVERAGE CHANGES in the incomes of different types of workers, but do not show what happens to the standard of living of individuals through time. It is possible, for example, for real wages in construction and manufacturing to remain constant while individuals improve their standards of living by moving from the construction sector to the industrial sector. Although changes in the production structure, which affect distribution through occupational mobility, can be captured by comparing estimates of the national income distribution, obtaining countrywide income data of comparable quality is not easy.

An alternative is to analyze occupational histories of individual households. This is difficult, however, in a country with high or variable inflation, such as Colombia, because people tend not to remember the exact date in the past when they earned a certain nominal wage.[1] Fortunately, however, we have found income data for a sample of poor and rich families in Cali based on a set of surveys of these families conducted throughout the 1970s.[2] This data set is exceptional, for as the *World Development Report 1978* states: "Very few [household surveys] follow the fortunes of individuals and families through time, or disaggregate the household to examine the well-being of women, children, and the elderly."[3]

The surveys were carried out as part of a study on nutrition by the Fundacion de Investigaciones de Ecologia Humana of Cali. They included information on income levels, quality of housing, education, and other socioeconomic indicators for a group of families living in one of the poorest squatter districts (Union de Vivienda Popular) of Cali in 1970. In addition, the researchers looked into the incomes and welfare indicators of a group of high-income families as a control group.[4]

The 1970 survey identified low-income families with children who showed signs of malnutrition. These children subsequently scored much lower in tests of cognitive ability than children from the sample of families at a high socioeconomic level. Nonetheless, the research and action program designed by the Fundacion de Ecologia Humana demonstrated that food supplements and psychological stimulation in special day-care centers for poor children enabled seven-year-olds who had been part of this program for four years to score measurably higher in tests of ability than children who were in the program for only one year, though these scores were still lower than those achieved by children of families at a high socioeconomic level.

Table 20 shows the general cognitive ability of the children in the sample and suggests the high cost to one's personal development of being born poor. It also indicates how programs to offset the disadvantages resulting from malnutrition and the lack of stimulation in childhood can help equalize the opportunities of individuals.

Characteristics of the Sample

For the purposes of this report, the important aspect of the research is that detailed information on the incomes and living conditions of a group of both low-income and high-income families in Cali was compiled in various years during a decade. Because it was possible to locate most of the

Table 20. *General Cognitive Ability of Rich and Poor Children in Cali, 1970*
(Average scaled scores)

		Average age (in months)				
Social group of children	Number of children	43	49	63	77	87
High income	28	−0.11	0.39	2.28	4.27	4.89
Low income						
Treated for 4 periods	50	−1.82	0.21	1.80	3.35	3.66
Treated for 3 periods	47	−1.72	−1.06	1.64	3.06	3.35
Treated for 2 periods	49	−1.94	−1.22	0.30	2.61	3.15
Treated for 1 period	90	−1.83	−1.11	0.33	2.07	2.73

Note: The higher the test scores, the better they are and the more cognitive ability they reflect. A treatment period is equivalent to a school year at the day-care center.

Source: Harrison McKay and others, "Improving Cognitive Ability in Chronically Deprived Children," Science, vol. 200 (April 21, 1978), p. 275.

same families in 1980, a final survey of most of them was carried out ten years later, to complete the history for a ten-year period.

The low-income families are a sample of the population in a district that was one of the poorest neighborhoods of Cali in 1970. The families were selected from a group with children born between June 1 and November 30, 1967; from this group, the children selected were those with the lowest weight and height, those with symptoms of clinical malnutrition, and those from families with the lowest incomes. The families were at the lowest quintile of the income distribution. The high-income families were within the highest 5 percent of the distribution.[5]

Table 21 compares selected characteristics of the high-income and low-income families in 1970. Clear differences are seen in the nutritional level of the children (as indicated by their weight and height), the education of their parents, and family income. Both the high-income families and the low-income families were relatively young in 1970: the average age of the father was thirty-seven and that of the mother thirty-one, while the number of family members under fifteen years of age was 4.8 for the poor and 2.4 for the rich.

Table 22 shows the number of families for which comparable information is available for each year. The 1980 survey was conducted especially for this study in the months of April and May.

Table 21. *Characteristics of Families in the Sample, 1970*

Variable	Low-income group	High-income group
Height of child as a percentage of normal for age	90	101
Weight of child as a percentage of normal for age	79	102
Per capita family income as a percentage of per capita family income of the rich	5	100
Per capita expenditure for food as a percentage of expenditure in rich families	15	100
Number of family members[a]	7.6	5.2
Number of members under 15 years of age	4.8	2.4
Number of playrooms and bedrooms per child	0.3	1.6
Average age of father	37	37
Average age of mother	31	31
Average years of education of father	3.6	14.5
Average years of education of mother	3.5	10.0

a. From Table 23.

Source: McKay and others, "Improving Cognitive Ability in Chronically Deprived Children."

Table 22. Number of Families for Which Usable Information Is Available, 1970–80

Item of information	1970 High income	1970 Low income	1974 High income	1974 Low income	1976 High income	1976 Low income	1980 High income	1980 Low income
Total income	37	176	35	159	34	171	34	152
Expenditures for food	37	175	35	162	33	173	37	168
Income of principal earner	37	176	35	161	32	171	28	152
Total families in survey	37	183	35	184	34	184	37	186

Note: Not all of the information from the available surveys could be used for each year because data are missing in some categories. In some cases, the expenditure reported for food is greater than total income, or figures are suspect (outliers). Such cases have been excluded for the analysis of the data.

Source: Fundación de Investigaciones de Ecología Humana (FIEH), Cali; and Fedesarrollo, Bogota.

Trends in the Real Income of Two Social Classes

The real family income and the per capita income of both socio-economic groups rose rapidly at a rate exceeding that of the national per capita income (see Table 23). The differential in family income between the rich and the poor improved to the benefit of the latter. Because of the greater increase in the number of persons per family in the low-income group, however, real per capita income increased less than family income, and less than the real per capita income of the wealthy families.[6] This illustrates how differences in family size between the two social classes favor the real consumption level of wealthy persons. However, the increase in family size may have been the means by which the poor added to their family income through the financial contribution made by all family members able to work.

Table 23. *Average Monthly Real Incomes of Rich and Poor Families in Cali, 1970–80*
(constant 1970 Colombian pesos)

Income group	1970	1974	1976	1980	Annual rate of increase, 1970–80 (percent)
High income					
Nominal family income	7,831	17,866	37,070	82,688	26.6
Real family income[a]	7,199	11,028	13,070	14,034	6.9
Nominal per capita income	1,513	3,489	7,596	16,705	27.0
Real per capita income[a]	1,395	2,153	2,678	2,835	7.3
Low income					
Nominal family income	748	1,654	2,562	9,865	29.4
Real family income[a]	728	929	909	1,546	7.8
Nominal per capita income	98	199	303	1,156	28.0
Real per capita income[a]	96	112	107	181	6.5
Income differentials					
Family (5 ÷ 1)	0.09	0.09	0.07	0.12	
Per capita (7 ÷ 3)	0.06	0.06	0.04	0.07	
Real national per capita income[b]	428	498	539	613[c]	3.7

a. For purposes of the present study, the base used was December 1970–100. Average real income is the nominal monthly income of each family, deflated by the Cali blue-collar consumer price index for the month in which the survey was made.

b. The figure used is that for December of the year closest to the month in which the survey was conducted. The base was 1970. *Source:* Banco de la Republica, national accounts. The annual income was divided by twelve to obtain a monthly estimate.

c. Fedesarrollo estimate.

Source: FIEH and Fedesarrollo sample.

One reason for the increase in family income has been the rise in the average number of persons working per family, especially among the poor (see Table 24). This increase is closely related to a significant rise in the participation of women and secondary workers in the labor force; moreover, the increase in participation has been greater in the low-income group.[7]

Finally, the data show that the increase in the number of women working did not contribute much to the rise in the family income of rich families because earnings of females in the high-income groups are low compared

Table 24. *Effect of Participation in the Labor Force on Incomes of the Rich and the Poor in Cali, 1970–80*

Income group	1970	1974	1976	1980
Average number of persons working per family				
High income	1.46	1.37	1.38	1.54
Low income	1.33	1.37	1.63	2.10
Average number of females working per family				
High income	0.32	0.29	0.38	0.56
Low income	0.24	0.28	0.46	0.68
Females working as a percentage of all females over 12 years of age				
High income	23	19	24	24
Low income	16	14	22	23
Average number of males working per family				
High income	1.13	1.08	1.00	0.97
Low income	1.07	1.08	1.16	1.42
Males working as a percentage of all males over 12 years of age				
High income	89	84	85	58
Low income	70	51	50	50
Average income of females as a percentage of average income of males				
High income	55	36	30	25
Low income	41	39	50	65
Average real income of head of household (Col $)[a]				
High income	5,652	9,728	10,230	12,360
Low income	646	760	695	916
Average real family income (Col $)[a]				
High income	7,199	11,028	13,070	14,034
Low income	728	929	909	1,546
Income of head of household as a percentage of total income				
High income	78	88	78	88
Low income	88	81	76	59

a. Deflators are Cali cost-of-living indexes for blue-collar workers.
Source: FIEH and Fedesarrollo sample.

with those of men and have decreased relatively throughout the decade. Among low-income families, in contrast, not only did the participation of females in the labor force increase, but their relative incomes rose as well.

The effect of participation in the labor force is shown in Table 24, in which it can be seen that the increase in the real incomes of heads of households in the high-income group was 119 percent during the decade, but was only 42 percent in the low-income group. During the same period, real family income rose 94 percent in the high-income group and 112 percent in the low-income group. It is clear, then, that the economic improvement of poor families has been due to the expansion of employment opportunities and to the higher earnings of secondary workers.

One of the most significant phenomena in the decade for the groups studied in Cali was the change in the participation of females in the labor force. Not only did female employment increase, but the gap between wages of females and males narrowed at lower skill levels.[8] The increased participation of women in the labor force could theoretically have been due to increasing poverty and male unemployment forcing women to enter the labor market. The increasing real wages of women and the decreasing income differential between the income of women and men, however, suggest that increasing labor demand was the determinant of higher participation rates. The hardship on both the working women and their children brought about by the increased participation in the labor force was probably not severe, because the families were large and there were other women in the household who could take care of the children and the housework. As Table 24 shows, by 1980 only 23 percent of females over the age of twelve from poor families were in the labor force.

Changes in Spending for Food

Changes in food consumption are a good indicator of changes in the welfare of low-income families. Table 25 shows how expenditure for food has changed among the two population groups studied. Both family groups increased their consumption of food during the period. This indicator is an excellent nutrition index for families at a higher socioeconomic level, inasmuch as the average number of persons per household declined. At the lower level, however, the average number of persons per household rose from 7.6 to 8.5 over the decade. As may be seen, real per capita expenditure for food rose among the low-income group, but the increase was concentrated in the second part of the decade.

Table 25. *Changes in the Expenditure on Food by Rich and Poor Families in Cali,*
1970–80
(Colombian pesos)

Income group	1970	1974	1976	1980
High income				
1. Nominal expenditure on food	2,584	4,942	7,876	18,946
2. Nominal family income	7,831	17,866	37,070	82,688
3. Real expenditure on food[a]	2,350	2,656	2,401	2,794
4. Real per capita expenditure on food	452	521	490	570
5. Row 1 as a percentage of row 2	32	28	21	23
Low income				
6. Nominal expenditure on food	579	1,055	1,702	5,423
7. Nominal family income	738	1,609	2,539	10,583
8. Real expenditure on food[a]	564	541	558	798
9. Real per capita expenditure on food	74	65	66	94
10. Row 6 as a percentage of row 7	79	65	67	51

Note: The income data in this table are slightly different from that in Table 23 because the data
on food expenditures were incomplete for some families where there were usable income data.
This table, therefore, covers a smaller number of families than are covered in Table 23.
    a. Real expenditure on food is nominal expenditure divided by the food price index for the
month of the survey.
Source: FIEH and Fedesarrollo sample.

Engel's law states that as a family's income rises, a smaller proportion of it
is spent on food. Moreover, a number of studies made in Latin America
suggest that urban families who spend more than 65 percent of their
income for food can be considered very poor and below the poverty
line.

The decline in the proportion of expenditure on food in both groups in
Cali confirms that real income has been rising, and the decline from 79
percent to 51 percent for the low-income group suggests that families are
moving out of absolute poverty levels. The table also shows, however, that
the real food expenditures of the poor deteriorated in the early 1970s and
improved substantially in the last part of the decade. Rapid increases in
food prices and the pressure to consume other goods, such as public
services, may explain the decrease in food expenditures in the first part of
the decade (see Figure 3).

Other Indicators of Welfare

The quality of housing and the access to public services are also good
indicators of welfare. In the case of the residents of the squatter district of

Figure 3. *Indicators Reflecting the Physical and Hygienic Quality of Dwellings of a Poor Neighborhood in Cali, 1970–80*

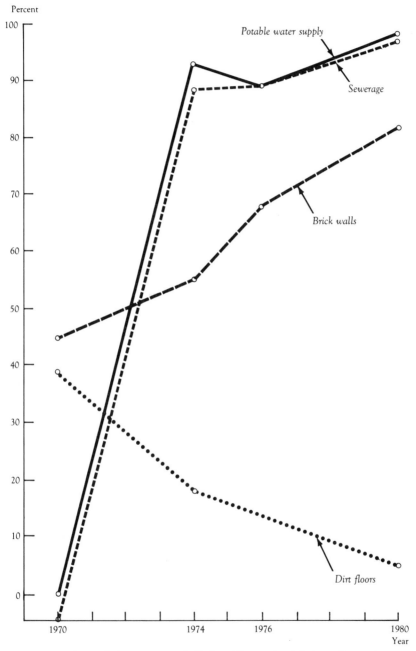

Source: Fundacion de Investigaciones de Ecologia Humana (FIEH)-Fedesarrollo sample.

Cali, the improvement in these indicators has been significant (see Figure 3). In 1970, no family had sewerage, but this service was available to 90 percent of the families by 1974 and 99 percent by 1980. Connections to potable water supply rose from 6 percent to 100 percent during the same period.

The decrease in the proportion of houses with dirt floors (42 percent to 9 percent) is another important improvement from the standpoint of health. The proportion of houses with brick walls also rose. Connection to the electricity system implies an increase in comfort, which is reflected in the fact that about 80 percent of the families were cooking with electric stoves in 1980 compared with 90 percent who cooked with oil in 1970.

Table 26 shows that as income rose, the poor families in Cali began to consume durable goods.[9] In 1976, for example, only 25 percent of these families owned refrigerators; by 1980, this proportion had risen to 48 percent. Ownership of a refrigerator is especially important from the standpoint of nutrition and comfort. In general, the consumption capacity of families like these seems to have increased over time, and they no longer constitute a negligible part of the market for domestic industry.

Government programs have made an obvious contribution to the improvement in the standard of living of this district. The local government has brought electricity, water, sewerage, and other services to the neighborhood at comparatively low prices, subsidized through higher connection charges and service rates in higher-income districts. Because the value of these services is greater than their cost to the user, this has contributed to an improvement in welfare.[10] The effect on health and nutrition of greater access to potable water and sewerage is clear. Electricity not only affords greater convenience but also, because of the time saved in performing

Table 26. *Percentage of Poor Families in Cali Possessing Selected Durable Goods, 1976–80*

Item	1976	1980	Percentage increase 1976–80
Refrigerator	25	48	93
Radio	82	83	2
Sewing machine	35	55	56
Television	31	72	132
Record player	16	27	73
Other[a]	—	91	—

—Data not available.
a. Including electric stoves, irons, and blenders.
Source: FIEH-Fedesarrollo sample.

household chores, provides the possibility for additional family members to seek employment.

Single-Parent Families

During the decade, a high percentage of both rich (21 percent) and poor (24 percent) families broke up. Average family income generally was lower in families where the father had left the household. Incomes of both the poor and the rich single-parent families were lower than the overall average for the respective social group (see Table 27). Moreover, the rate of annual increase in the total incomes of the single-parent rich families was lower than the average for all rich families. Although single-parent poor families have lower incomes than the average for all poor families, their real incomes rose more rapidly than the average among poor families because the earnings of women and secondary workers in this social class grew so rapidly.[11] In other words, because the incomes that increased most were those of wives and because secondary workers were able to find employment, single-parent poor families saw an improvement in their relative situations during the decade. This phenomenon probably helped to alleviate significantly problems of extreme poverty.

Table 27. *Average Monthly Incomes of the Rich and the Poor Single-Parent Families in Cali, 1970–80*
(Colombian pesos)

Income by social group	1970	1974	1976	1980	Annual rates of growth (percent)
Nominal family income					
High income	7,210	8,800	16,250	46,989	20.6
Low income	466	1,257	2,241	8,961	34.4
Real family income[a]					
High income	6,637	5,403	5,610	7,975	1.8
Low income	461	688	795	1,401	11.8
Family income of single-parent family as percentage of average family income					
High income	92	49	44	57	
Low income	62	76	87	91	

a. Real family income is nominal income deflated by the Cali consumer price index for blue-collar workers (low-income families) and white-collar workers (in the case of high-income families).

Source: FIEH and Fedesarrollo sample.

Occupational Mobility

Analysis of the employment history of the sample does not suggest much upward or downward mobility. There are cases such as that of the head of household who declared in 1970 that his occupation was "whatever turns up"; in 1974 he was a warehouse worker, in 1976 a fruit seller, and in 1980 a tradesman. Most individuals, however, remain in the same occupational category over time. In other words, the rise in income in the low socioeconomic group resulted more from increases in the number of family members in the labor force and from higher earnings than from the occupational mobility of the father or the mother over time.

Table 28 uses a broader definition than usual to measure mobility. In some studies, a person is considered to have ascended on the occupational scale only when he moves from laborer to clerk, or from self-employed worker to owner. In the present case, a person was considered to have ascended if he moved from caretaker to production worker, or from street peddler to industrial worker. Even with this broad criterion, however, it is clear from the table that there was little occupational mobility.

Table 28. *Measurements of Occupational Mobility, 1970–80*
(number of workers)

Social group	Males	Females
High income		
Upward mobility[a]	2	1
Downward mobility	1	0
Total workers[b]	29	12
Low income		
Upward mobility	30	5
Downward mobility	6	1
Total workers[b]	129	68

Note: The measurement is rather subjective. A street peddler who has become a miner is considered to have ascended, as has a warehouseman who has become a production worker; a bricklayer who becomes a doorman is not regarded as having changed occupational level, nor a street peddler who becomes a "trader." Although the occupations of people at the various sample dates were looked at to get an idea of the occupational history of individuals, the figures in the table reflect changes in occupation between 1970 and 1980.

a. Movement from professional to managerial status.

b. Persons working in 1980.

Source: FIEH and Fedesarrollo sample.

Comparison of Income Data from the Survey and Wage Series

Table 29 compares the income data from the sample with information from DANE on salaries and wages of manufacturing, construction, and agricultural workers in the Cauca Valley and in Cali. In 1970, the incomes of heads of households in the poor neighborhood were higher than those of agricultural daily workers, but lower than those of construction workers

Table 29. *Comparison of Average Nominal Monthly Salaries and Wages in Selected Industries and Incomes of Heads of Selected Households in Cali, 1970–80*
(nominal Colombian pesos)

Sector	1970[a]	1974[b]	1976[c]	1980
Manufacturing industry (Cauca Valley)				
Executive and technical personnel	6,683	9,940	16,484	37,600[d]
Clerks	2,650	4,242	5,876	13,400
Laborers	1,294	2,054	3,191	7,900
Apprentices	517	1,119	1,973	
Construction (Cali)[e]	932	1,203	1,758	5,600[f]
Agriculture (Cauca Valley)	435	—	1,650	4,350[g]
Sample (Cali) heads of household.				
High income	6,165	15,771	28,756	72,803
Low income	653	1,361	1,949	5,861

—Data not available.

Note: The comparison is between the FIEH-Fedesarrollo sample of families with the information collected from DANE surveys.

a. For industry, average monthly salaries and wages are for 1970; for construction, the average wage is for December 1971; for agriculture, the average daily wage is for 1970 (the wage is for men in hot-climate areas, with no food provided).

b. For industry, average monthly salaries and wages are for 1974; for construction, the average wage is for the first four months of 1974.

c. For industry, average monthly salaries and wages are for 1976; for construction, the average wage is for the months of May, June, July, and August.

d. The estimate is based on the data from the monthly manufacturing survey for March 1980.

e. Average for masters, journeymen, and helpers. Calculated from DANE data using average wages in Cali for each category in December 1979, assigning them weights of 10 percent, 43 percent, and 47 percent, respectively, in the total, and applying this value to the index of construction labor costs in Cali.

f. Average for March and April 1980.

g. Daily agricultural wage (in hot climate, with no food provided), during the fourth quarter of 1979.

Source: DANE, Annual Survey of Manufacturing (various issues) and *Monthly Statistical Bulletin,* FIEH-Fedesarrollo sample.

or industrial laborers. This was to be expected, and the comparison confirms the high quality of the survey information. The workers in the sample are concentrated in occupations in the urban informal sector, which should generate higher earnings than farm work to justify rural-urban migration; however, incomes are lower than those of occupations in the formal sector of the economy, such as industry or construction, although the latter is quite similar to urban informal employment. By the end of the decade, the incomes of the low-income sample were higher than those of construction workers.

The incomes of the high-income sample were close to the average income declared by industrial executives and technicians in 1970. At the end of the decade, however, most of the highly skilled persons in the sample were above the levels of industrial executives, which placed the group at the top of the distribution.

Also significant is the reduction in the dispersion of income among the working class. The differential between daily wages in agriculture and those in construction declined over the 1970s, as did the differential between rural wages and income earned in the urban informal sector (represented here by the low-income sample). The period also saw a closing of the gap between industrial laborers and informal sector workers.[12] This reduction in income differentials within the working class indicates a decrease in the dualism in the economy, which in turn may be related to the lessening of protection for the formal sector of the urban economy.

During the 1970s, the real incomes of the upper-class group rose at a rapid rate of 9 percent a year (see Table 30). Over that period, the real incomes of the heads of households from the poor neighborhood rose at an average annual rate of 3.5 percent, which was greater than the increase in the incomes of construction workers and manufacturing industry employees (the real incomes of the latter did not improve), but less than the rise in agricultural wages.

These results help to confirm the hypothesis that there was a redistribution of income toward the two extremes of the population during the decade. The incomes of the poorest groups—the landless *campesinos* and female urban workers in the informal sector—increased faster than per capita income, and at rates matching those for professionals and businessmen. Consequently, industrial wages paid in the formal sector of the economy have lost ground in relation to wages in the informal sector or to wages of unskilled workers and *campesinos*. Heads of poor urban households, however, probably did not improve their relative position in the income distribution because their incomes grew, according to Table 30, at about the same rate as the per capita national income.

Table 30. *Comparison of Average Real Monthly Salaries and Wages in Selected Industries and Incomes of Heads of Selected Households in Cali, 1970–80*
(constant 1970 Colombian pesos)

Sector	1970	1974	1976	1980	Annual rate of increase
Manufacturing industry					
Executive and technical personnel	7,035	5,616	6,290	6,530	−0.7
Clerical workers	2,790	2,397	2,240	2,325	−1.8
Laborers	1,360	1,087	1,130	1,270	−0.7
Apprentices	545	592	700		
Construction	785	730	630	900	1.7
Agriculture	458	—	569	700	4.3
Sample of household heads					
High income	5,652	9,728	10,230	13,393	9.0
Low income	646	760	695	916	3.5

—Data not available.
Note: The comparison is between the FIEH-Fedesarrollo sample of families with the information collected from DANE surveys.
Source: Table 29, deflated by the consumer price index for Cali (1970=100).

In absolute terms, although the average incomes of heads of lower-class households rose during the period, in 1980 they remained below the average for industrial laborers. In contrast, for the upper class represented in the sample, the average income in 1970 was lower than that of the executive and technical personnel in industry, but was twice as high in 1980.[13] This means that in 1980 the groups of the sample remained at the extremes of the distribution.

Conclusion

The research conducted in Cali documents the movement of income levels and welfare indicators for two groups of families at the extremes of the income distribution in the 1970s. This exercise leads to several important conclusions.

• During the 1970s, income was redistributed toward those at the top and the bottom of the income distribution. The real per capita incomes of both the rich and the poor families rose at an average rate exceeding that of the per capita national income. Similarly, the incomes of heads of households in these groups rose during the period when real salaries and wages in the manufacturing industry were declining or growing very slowly.

• The real family incomes of both the poor and the rich increased significantly. The rise in the incomes of the poor seems to be due primarily to increases in the average number of family members who work and in the earnings of the wife and secondary workers, whereas among the rich, the increase in the income of the head of household explains most of the rise in total income.

• Single-parent families in both social classes have lower incomes than the average for all families in their class, but the income gains for single-parent poor families were substantial. This phenomenon probably helped to decrease the incidence of absolute poverty because many of the poorest families are of this nature.

None of these trends is inconsistent with the evidence presented in Chapter 2 on wage trends. On the contrary, the data on the large gains in earnings of unskilled and informal-sector workers in a poor area of Cali are consistent with the evidence on real wage increases for agricultural workers since there is probably much mobility between the two sectors. However, the low growth rate of earnings of workers in the formal sector is clearly not a good proxy for the earnings of the poor or of workers in the informal sector during the 1970s. Even within the informal sector, the earnings of secondary workers grew faster than those of household heads. All evidence, then, points toward a decrease in the dispersion of labor earnings in the economy.

The data from the Cali sample also suggest that the commonly available statistics on wages in large industries may be misleading and that the stagnation in earnings of this sector, which in fact represents the middle class, may be consistent with an improvement in the standard of living for the lower deciles of the income distribution.

The evidence from the wage series together with the income data from the Cali sample indicate that during the 1970s there was a reduction in poverty and that the gap between the formal and informal sectors diminished. It may be that this happened to some extent at the expense of the middle class.

This deterioration in the relative position of the middle class may have profound political implications. To what extent, for example, has this phenomenon affected the trends toward a decrease in voter participation, the creation of urban political fringe movements that do not reject violent tactics, and a general dissatisfaction among intellectuals with the performance of the country's economic and political institutions? These questions are difficult to answer here.

In the next chapter, evidence from household surveys will be shown to confirm the general trends described in this chapter. It is, however, clear from a careful analysis that the income distribution in Colombia has not become more skewed during the country's successful economic development effort of the last fifteen years. This runs counter to the common impression, because the people who write about Colombian economic policy belong to precisely the class that has seen no clear improvement in its standard of living.

Notes to Chapter 3

1. It is for this reason that occupational histories are regarded as unreliable. See Bernardo Kugler, Alvaro Reyes, and Maria Isabel de Gomez, *Educacion y Mercado de Trabajo Urbano en Colombia: Una Comparacion entre Sectores Moderno y no Moderno*, monograph 10 (Bogota: Corporacion Centro Regional de Poblacion, 1979).

2. Cali is Colombia's third largest city and the capital of the department of Valle del Cauca.

3. World Bank, *World Development Report 1978* (New York: Oxford University Press, 1978).

4. Harrison Mckay and others, "Improving Cognitive Ability in Chronically Deprived Children," *Science*, vol. 200 (April 21, 1978).

5. The average family income of the wealthiest 10 percent in Cali in 1968 was Col$4,900 a month; see Philip Musgrove, *Consumer Behavior in Latin America* (Washington, D.C.: Brookings Institution, 1978). The 1968 figure is equivalent to Col$5,494 a month in 1970 when correction is made for increases in the cost of living over two years. This figure compares with an average family income of Col$7,831 for the high-income group in our sample for that year. The rich families were chosen from a group of families headed by professionals, who had babies born between June and November 1967.

6. In the upper class, the average number of persons per family declined from 5.2 in 1970 to 4.9 in 1980; in the lower class, it increased from 7.6 to 8.5 persons. The average number of children under fifteen years of age fell by 17 percent in both cases, although the total number of children in poor families continued to be roughly twice that in rich families. These findings may indicate that in low-income families children remain at home for a longer period after they have reached working age; this in turn may be associated with the need for a larger number of persons working in order to augment household income.

7. In both social classes, the total number of females working has increased more than that of males. This is reflected in an increase both in the average number of females working per family and in the rate of participation of females (see Table 24). In the case of males, the average number of workers per family rose in the lower class but fell in the upper class, while the rate of male participation declined in both cases.

8. According to the data from the Social Security Institute, the average salary of females covered by the programs of that institution was 68 percent of the average salary of males in 1970. By 1978, the proportion had risen to 74 percent.

9. Information on durable goods is available only for 1976 and 1980. Furthermore, the data only allow comparison of the possession of refrigerators, radios, sewing machines, television sets, and record players. In 1980, questions were included about electric stoves, irons, blenders, and other appliances, but comparable information is not available for the earlier period.

10. The value of one gallon of water to the user is greater than the cost charged per gallon by the public utility company. This is evidenced by the fact that in districts without a water supply, families purchase water from trucks at prices much higher than those charged by the water supply system.

11. As may be seen in Table 24, the share of the income of the head of household in total family income for rich families increased from 78 percent in 1970–71 to 88 percent in 1980, whereas among the poor that share was 88 percent in 1970–71 and fell to 59 percent in 1980.

12. It can be argued that it is not correct to compare changes in average wages through time with changes in the incomes of individuals, because the latter reflect increases in age and experience, which the average wage data do not reflect in a rapidly growing population. Experience probably explains why in 1980 the incomes of the household heads of rich families are above the average incomes of executives. Experience, on the other hand, affects much less the wages of rural laborers or low-skilled self-employed workers. For that reason, it does not seem inadequate to compare the average wages of unskilled workers with the income of the heads of poor households in our sample.

13. This shows the high slope of the earnings curve of managerial personnel between the ages of thirty-seven and forty-seven. Casual observation suggests that this type of earnings curve, in fact, reflects the job history of upper-class professionals in Colombia.

4

The Evidence from
Household Surveys

ESTIMATES OF INCOME DISTRIBUTION in most countries generally are based
on data from household surveys. Income data from these surveys are often
unreliable, however, and it is particularly difficult to compare distributions
based on surveys carried out at different times and with different
methodologies. In the case of Colombia, a simple comparison of
concentration ratios derived from different household surveys is not valid
because of large variations in the quality and coverage of the surveys.

This chapter presents the results of different household surveys and
attempts to derive a distribution for 1971–72 comparable to that calculated
by the author in 1964. In addition, an effort is made to compare income
distributions from surveys of similar quality at the start and at the end of
the decade of the 1970s.

Between 1970 and 1980, DANE carried out twenty-seven household
surveys (EH). At the start of the decade, some of these were expenditure
surveys, and consumption and income information was gathered with some
care.[1] Other surveys dealt primarily with the labor force; their questions
concerning income were fewer and more general, and for that reason they
underestimated income more than the expenditure surveys.[2]

Even the higher-quality household surveys appear to underestimate
income significantly if one compares the resulting income distributions with
data from national accounts, which in turn probably underestimate the true
level of per capita income in Colombia. The more disaggregated income
data from the surveys indicate that the underestimation of rural income is
quite high and that the information from the urban areas covers primarily
labor income. Household surveys tend not to capture income from capital
and land in the countryside or part of capital income in urban areas.
Because of the large proportion of owner-operated farms in Colombia, the

degree of underestimation of rural incomes in household surveys is substantial.

Table 31 shows estimates of the degree of underreporting of income in five household surveys and in the population census. Labor force surveys clearly have a higher degree of underestimation than expenditure surveys such as that of 1971, and the census contains the least reliable data. Furthermore, a survey such as EH-4 (1971) certainly cannot be compared with EH-19 (1978). The degree of underreporting of rural incomes also suggests the need to generate a rural income distribution with statistical material other than that obtained from household surveys.

In addition to the official household surveys, two private surveys were also carried out during the decade. The first was a national income and expenditure survey in 1974; the second was a 1977 survey carried out in four cities by the Centro de Estudios para el Desarrollo Economico (CEDE) of the Universidad de los Andes for a research project on poverty and employment.[3] The information from the latter probably gives quite accurate data on labor income of the poor in the largest cities, but the data on the incomes of the upper five deciles of the distribution seem to have serious errors of underestimation.

Finally, because the rural income data derived from household surveys were unreliable, an effort was made to find agricultural production and income information from production surveys. Although there have been various attempts to measure income and production at the farm level, these studies are often confined to small geographical areas. The one national survey carried out by DANE had so many problems of coverage and inconsistencies that it was never published.[4] Furthermore, in the 1970s, DANE did not carry out any agricultural production surveys such as those on which Berry and Padilla based the rural income distribution of 1960.[5]

Nevertheless, an interesting agricultural production survey was carried out by the Colombian Central Bank in 1972 to determine how credit was distributed in the countryside and what relation existed between credit availability and productivity. This survey is used here to estimate an agricultural income distribution similar to that used in the Urrutia-Berry distribution of income for 1964.[6]

Changes in Income Distribution between 1964 and 1972

The earliest reliable income distribution for Colombia is for 1964. The methodology used to arrive at that distribution is described in detail in the 1970 work by Berry and Padilla and in the 1975 study by Urrutia and Berry.

Table 31. *Percentage of Personal Income Accounted for in Various Household Surveys, 1970–78*

Income[a]	EH-1 June 1970	EH-3 April 1971	EH-4[b] July 1971	EH-5 November 1971	Census 1973	Selowsky 1974	EH-19 April 1978
Rural income	48	36	81	40	20	50	36
Urban income	—	—	77	—	—	—	70
Total income	—	—	78	51	51.4	—	65

—Data not available.

Note: EH stands for household surveys.

a. Total personal income was derived from national accounts.

b. Expenditure surveys.

Source: For EH-4 and EH-19, special tabulations of the DANE surveys. For EH-1, EH-3, EH-5, and Census, the source is DANE; 1974 data is from Marcelo Selowsky, *Who Benefits from Government Expenditure? A Case Study of Colombia* (New York: Oxford University Press, 1979).

This section will first summarize the statistical sources used to generate the 1964 distribution as a basis for understanding the methodology used for the 1972 estimate.

Because rural household surveys were unavailable in the 1960s, the rural income distribution was calculated from four sources: the population census, data on value-added for farms of different sizes based on an agricultural production survey, information on wages of agricultural laborers, and data on the distribution of farms by size based on the 1960 census of agricultural production units. In other words, the agricultural income distribution reflects closely the distribution of land, corrected for the difference in average value-added by size of farms. To this distribution were added the distribution of income of landless laborers and the wage income of owners of small plots who work part of the year for wages. To obtain a rural income distribution, a special estimate of nonagricultural income in rural areas was added to the agricultural distribution.[7]

The urban income distribution for 1964 was derived primarily from the urban labor force surveys of CEDE, particularly those published in a 1969 study by Isaza and Ortega, but also those carried out in small cities in 1963.[8] The incomes of agricultural workers living in the cities were subtracted from the urban distribution because this income was presumably captured at the farm level. Various additional adjustments included the imputation of income paid in kind for workers in domestic services and the increase of labor income by the equivalent of minimum legal fringe benefits, a type of income not clearly identified in the labor force surveys.

The methodology used for obtaining a rural income distribution in 1964 clearly covers income from capital and land. It may, in fact, overestimate the concentration of income in agriculture by assigning all of the income from a large farm to one owner, even though large farms often support wholly or in part the families of various brothers and sisters. Furthermore, the value-added method of estimating net income probably leaves out some minor costs of production that may add up to significant amounts. For all these reasons, not only is the concentration of income calculated for the rural sector of Colombia in 1964 higher than any of the estimates that are based solely on household surveys, but also the Gini coefficient is higher than that found for the rural sector of many other countries.[9] The main reason for the higher rural inequality found for 1964 is that the methodology used probably covers most capital income and rents from land, whereas most household surveys seriously underestimate these types of income.

To calculate a comparable agricultural income distribution for 1972, we used the value-added data by farm size derived from a Banco de la

Republica survey on agricultural credit.[10] Information from this survey, in combination with data from the 1970–71 agricultural census, data on daily wages of agricultural workers, and labor force data from the 1973 population census, allowed us to calculate an agricultural income distribution with a similar methodology to that used by Berry to obtain the 1964 distribution.[11] Table 32 shows the agricultural income distribution for 1972.

To obtain the rural income distribution, the income distribution of nonagricultural rural workers based on the DANE July 1971 household survey (EH-4) was added to the figures in Table 32, after adjusting for the difference in dates of the 1972 Banco survey and the EH-4 household survey. This rural distribution for 1972 is summarized in Table 33.[12] Like the 1964 distribution, the one for 1972 probably overestimates to some extent the concentration of rural incomes because of an exaggeration of capital income in large farms and because all the capital income of large farms is assigned to only one person. In addition, in 1972 large farms seem to be overrepresented in the sample used.

The Gini coefficient for the rural distribution of 1972 is 0.63, while that for 1964 was 0.58. As Table 34 shows, however, our estimate shows much more concentration of income than is shown by the Selowsky survey of 1974 or the DANE expenditure survey of 1971. Clearly, these last two estimates do not cover a significant part of capital income and may underestimate significantly the income of farmers who derived their income from their own land.

The urban income distribution for 1972 was also calculated with the methodology used in 1964. The EH-4 (1971) household expenditure survey was used to derive the urban distribution for the economically active population. Because the EH-4 data are for family income, it was necessary to use the original data to obtain an urban income distribution for each economically active person. Persons deriving their income from agriculture but living in cities were taken out of this distribution because presumably their income is recorded in the rural distribution. The resulting distribution was then adjusted for population growth, changes in income per capita, and prices for 1971–72 to arrive at a 1972 urban income distribution, which, when added to Table 33, produced the national income distribution found in Table 35.

The urban distribution for 1972 has a Gini coefficient of 0.54 compared with 0.48 obtained in 1964. Although for 1972 no adjustment was made for the incomes paid in kind for domestic service, and such an adjustment would decrease income dispersion, it still appears that in the urban sector the income distribution deteriorated between 1964 and 1972. Table 36

Table 32. Distribution of Personal Income Obtained from Agricultural Work, 1972

Annual income (Colombian pesos)	Number of persons (thousands)	Percentage of persons	Total income (millions of Colombian pesos)	Percentage of income	Accumulated percentage of persons	Accumulated percentage of income
0–2,000	46.5	2.24	80	0.16	2.24	0.16
2,001–4,000	133.6	6.43	434	0.85	8.67	1.01
4,001–6,000	170.8	8.22	906	1.77	16.89	2.78
6,001–8,000	248.2	11.95	1,791	3.50	28.84	6.28
8,001–10,000	538.4	25.91	4,883	9.55	54.75	15.83
10,001–12,000	195.7	9.42	2,137	4.18	64.17	20.01
12,001–14,000	78.3	3.77	1,053	2.05	67.94	22.06
14,001–16,000	182.8	8.80	2,685	5.25	76.74	27.31
16,001–22,000	123.4	5.94	2,414	4.72	82.68	32.03
22,001–28,000	114.0	5.49	2,948	5.77	88.17	37.80
28,001–36,000	47.8	2.30	1,519	2.97	90.47	40.77
36,001–48,000	64.3	3.09	2,745	5.37	93.56	46.14
48,001–60,000	30.9	1.49	1,640	3.21	95.05	49.35

60,001–72,000	12.7	0.61	829	1.62	95.66	50.97
72,001–84,000	12.9	0.62	985	1.93	96.28	52.90
84,001–96,000	4.9	0.24	441	0.86	96.52	53.76
96,001–108,000	13.0	0.62	1,317	2.58	97.14	56.34
108,001–120,000	1.7	0.08	204	0.40	97.22	56.74
120,001–144,000	8.7	0.42	1,056	2.06	97.64	58.80
144,001–180,000	7.8	0.38	1,297	2.54	98.02	61.34
180,001–240,000	13.3	0.64	2,812	5.50	98.66	66.84
240,001–360,000	14.9	0.72	4,272	8.35	99.38	75.19
360,001–480,000	0.6	0.03	232	0.45	99.41	75.64
480,001–600,000	4.6	0.22	2,393	4.68	99.63	80.32
600,001–720,000	2.2	0.10	1,609	3.15	99.73	83.47
720,001–840,000	1.9	0.09	1,396	2.73	99.82	86.20
840,001–960,000	0.7	0.03	607	1.19	99.85	87.39
960,001 or more	3.1	0.15	6,452	12.61	100.00	100.00
Total	2,077.7	100.0	51,135	100.0		

Note: The figures do not include family workers.

Source: Clara Elsa de Sandoval and Miguel Urrutia, "Distribucion del Ingreso Proveniente de la Actividad Agropecuaria en Colombia" (Bogota: Fedesarrollo, November 1980; processed).

Table 33. Rural Income Distribution, 1972

Annual income (Colombian pesos)	Number of persons (thousands)	Percentage of persons	Accumulated percentage of persons	Total income (millions of Colombian pesos)	Percentage of income	Accumulated percentage of income
0–4,000	263.0	10.65	10.65	654	1.15	1.15
4,001–6,000	233.2	9.44	20.09	1,208	2.13	3.28
6,001–10,000	838.4	33.94	54.03	7,122	12.56	15.84
10,001–12,000	195.7	7.92	61.95	2,137	3.77	19.61
12,001–14,000	124.5	5.04	66.99	1,601	2.82	22.43
14,001–16,000	229.5	9.29	76.28	3,412	6.02	28.45
16,001–22,000	144.9	5.87	82.15	2,827	4.99	33.44
22,001–28,000	157.4	6.37	88.52	3,993	7.04	40.48
28,001–36,000	61.4	2.49	91.01	1,918	3.38	43.86
36,001–48,000	79.6	3.22	94.23	3,366	5.94	49.80
48,001–60,000	33.5	1.36	95.59	1,778	3.14	52.94
60,001–72,000	12.7	0.51	96.10	829	1.46	54.44
72,001–84,000	16.3	0.66	96.76	1,247	2.20	56.60

84,001–96,000	5.3	0.21	96.97	477	0.84	57.44
96,001–120,000	15.3	0.62	97.59	1,579	2.79	60.23
120,001–144,000	9.1	0.37	97.96	1,105	1.95	62.18
144,001–180,000	7.8	0.32	98.28	1,297	2.29	64.47
180,001–240,000	14.8	0.60	98.88	3,174	5.60	70.07
240,001–360,000	14.9	0.60	99.48	4,272	7.54	77.61
360,001–480,000	0.6	0.02	99.50	232	0.41	78.02
480,001–600,000	4.6	0.19	99.69	2,393	4.22	82.24
600,001–720,000	2.2	0.09	99.78	1,609	2.84	85.08
720,001–840,000	1.9	0.08	99.86	1,396	2.46	87.54
840,001–960,000	0.7	0.03	99.89	607	1.07	88.61
960,001 or more	3.1	0.13	100.02	6,452	11.38	99.99
Total	2,470.4	100.02		56,683	99.99	

Source: Total agricultural distribution obtained from the Banco de la Republica farm sample for 1972, plus the income distribution of nonagricultural workers obtained from EH-4 (1971). This last distribution was transformed to 1972 pesos using a consumer price index, a population growth rate, and an estimate of growth in income per capita between the two dates.

Table 34. *Various Rural Income Distribution Studies, 1964–74*
(accumulated percentage of income)

Accumulated percentage of economically active persons who receive income	Urrutia-Berry 1964	EH-4 1971	EH-4 adjustment[a] 1971	Urrutia-Sandoval 1972	Deciles by per capita family income	Selowsky 1974[b]
10	0.9	1.5	1.1	1.2	10	3.0
20	4.2	3.8	3.4	3.6	20	7.6
30	8.5	8.0	7.0	5.5	30	13.8
40	13.5	13.2	11.5	9.5	40	20.9
50	19.0	19.0	16.0	15.0	50	29.8
60	26.0	26.0	22.0	18.5	60	38.6
70	34.0	35.0	29.5	25.0	70	47.5
80	45.0	46.5	38.5	32.5	80	59.4
90	59.5	60.0	52.0	43.0	90	73.5
95	—	71.5	63.0	53.0	95	81.9
100	100.0	100.0	100.0	100.0	100	100.0
Gini coefficient	0.58	0.49	0.56	0.63		0.32

a. The adjustment consisted of assigning all of the 19 percent calculated underestimation of rural incomes to the top 10 percent of the population. This is an extreme assumption, but it is based on the supposition that the household survey does not capture capital income.

b. Accumulated by deciles of per capita family income.

Source: For EH-4, DANE; Miguel Urrutia and Albert Berry, *La Distribucion del Ingreso en Colombia* (Medellin: Editorial la Carreta, 1975); de Sandoval and Urrutia, "Distribucion del Ingreso Proveniente"; Selowsky, *Who Benefits from Government Expenditure?*

shows that the seventh to the ninth deciles of the population—that is, the middle class—and the tenth decile improved their positions at the expense of the lower six deciles.

The national income distribution changed little between 1964 and 1972 (see Table 37). If anything, the top and the bottom of the distribution gained a little, but the changes are insignificant. This is reflected in similar Gini coefficients—0.57 for 1964 and 0.58 for 1972.

Since the 1972 agricultural distribution may overestimate the income from large farms, it is possible to state with some confidence that the distribution of income did not become more unequal between 1964 and 1972. By themselves, however, both the rural and the urban distributions were less equal in 1972, so that any partial analysis would suggest a concentration of income. But a closing of the gap between rural and urban incomes avoided a worsening in the national income distribution.

Table 35. National Income Distribution, 1972

Annual income (Colombian pesos)	Number of persons (thousands)	Percentage of persons	Accumulated percentage of persons	Total income (millions of Colombian pesos)	Percentage of income	Accumulated percentage of income
0–4,000	567.4	10.32	10.32	1,128	0.91	0.91
4,001–6,000	580.3	10.55	20.87	2,640	2.12	3.03
6,001–10,000	1,162.8	21.15	42.02	9,410	7.55	10.58
10,001–14,000	623.4	11.34	53.36	6,706	5.38	15.96
14,001–16,000	522.2	9.50	62.86	7,147	5.73	21.69
16,001–22,000	564.1	10.26	73.12	10,030	8.05	29.74
22,001–36,000	610.7	11.11	84.23	15,341	12.31	42.05
36,001–48,000	337.6	6.14	90.37	12,076	9.69	51.74
48,001–60,000	127.9	2.33	92.70	5,972	4.79	56.53
60,001–72,000	67.8	1.23	93.93	3,718	2.98	59.51
72,001–84,000	88.0	1.60	95.53	5,714	4.58	64.09
84,001–96,000	29.8	0.54	96.07	2,219	1.78	65.87
96,001–120,000	58.9	1.07	97.14	5,185	4.16	70.03
120,001–144,000	36.4	0.66	97.80	3,917	3.14	73.17
144,001–180,000	42.6	0.77	98.57	5,697	4.57	77.74
180,001–240,000	20.5	0.37	98.94	4,120	3.31	81.05
240,001 or more	58.3	1.06	100.00	23,629	18.96	100.01
Total	5,498.7	100.0		124,648	100.01	

Source: De Sandoval and Urrutia, "Distribucion del Ingreso Proveniente."

Table 36. *Urban Income Distribution of the Employed Population Excluding Farmers Living in Cities, 1964–1971*
(percent of total income in decile)

Decile of economically active population	1964	1971
1	0.9	1.1
2	3.3	1.4
3	4.3	2.8
4	5.0	3.7
5	5.5	4.5
6	7.0	6.5
7	8.0	8.5
8	11.0	11.0
9	14.5	17.0
10	40.5	43.0

Source: Urrutia and Berry, *La Distribucion del Ingreso en Colombia*; and de Sandoval and Urrutia, "Distribucion del Ingreso Proviente."

Table 37. *National Income Distribution, 1964 and 1972*
(percent of total income in decile)

Decile of economically active population	1964	1972
1	1.1	0.9
2	1.4	2.1
3	2.8	3.0
4	3.7	3.5
5	4.5	5.0
6	5.5	5.5
7	8.0	7.0
8	10.0	10.5
9	15.0	13.5
10	48.0	49.0

Source: Urrutia and Berry, *La Distribucion del Ingreso en Colombia*; and de Sandoval and Urrutia, "Distribucion del Ingreso Proveniente."

Table 36 is consistent with the wage series analyzed in Chapter 2, which showed that the 1960s had been a period of rapid gains in real earnings for the middle class. This is reflected in the increasing share of total urban income received by the top four deciles of the urban distribution. Table 38 on rural income distribution is also consistent with the observed increase in agricultural wages, because in absolute terms the income of the lower deciles increased significantly, although less rapidly than that of the wealthy landowners and rural entrepreneurs. The rapid rate of growth in Colombia's rural areas, where most poverty was concentrated in 1964, explains why the national income distribution did not deteriorate despite growing inequality in both the rural and the urban areas.

Alternative Comparison of Changes in Income Distribution in the 1960s

An alternative to the 1964–72 comparison made earlier is to compare the EH-4 national expenditure survey, which is of high quality, with the 1964 income distribution. Table 39 shows that the Gini coefficients in these two distributions are similar, confirming the impression that the distribution of income did not become more unequal. However, the methodology for obtaining rural incomes is quite different in the two distributions; the 1964 methodology produces higher incomes for large farmers.

Table 39, however, does show that the middle class received a greater share of total income in 1971 than in 1964. This had been suggested by the wage series presented in Chapter 2. The table also supports the results of the 1964–72 comparison discussed earlier, in the sense that it shows no deterioration in the distribution of income over the decade of the 1960s.

Changes in Income Distribution between 1971 and 1978

No survey of agricultural production is available for the end of the 1970s and, therefore, the 1964 methodology cannot be used. The only comparison possible is between the distributions derived from household surveys. Because the only national survey at the end of the decade is DANE's EH-19 for April 1978, that survey must be compared with one of similar quality at the beginning of the decade.

Table 38. Changes in Agricultural Income by Decile, 1960–72

Decile of economically active population	Berry 1960		Percentage of income	1972 estimate		Increase in annual per capita income (percent) [a]
	Percentage of income	Average income (1960 Colombian pesos)		Average income (1972 Colombian pesos)	Average income at constant 1960 prices	
1	2.24	865	1.5	3,691	1,079	1.9
2	2.87	1,110	2.0	4,922	1,439	2.2
3	3.34	1,290	3.0	7,383	2,259	4.3
4	3.73	1,440	3.2	7,876	2,303	3.9
5	4.21	1,625	3.8	9,351	2,734	4.4
6	4.68	1,807	4.5	11,073	3,238	4.9
7	5.78	2,232	5.0	12,304	3,598	4.0
8	7.90	3,060	7.0	17,225	5,036	4.2
9	12.77	4,940	10.8	26,576	7,771	3.8
10	52.48	20,270	59.2	145,697	42,601	6.4
Total	100.0	3,830	100.0	24,611	7,196	5.4

a. Annual geometric growth rate, 1960–72.
Source: Albert Berry and Alfonso Padilla, "La Distribucion de Ingresos Provenientes de la Agricultura en Colombia, 1960" Universidad Nacional, Documento de Trabajo (Bogota: CID, January/March 1970); and de Sandoval and Urrutia, "Distribucion del Ingreso Proveniente."

Table 39. *Comparison of Two Income Distribution Estimates, 1964 and 1971*

Decile of the economically active population	1964		1971	
	Percentage of rural income	*Percentage of total income*	*Percentage of rural income*	*Percentage of total income*
1	1.4	1.1	1.5	1.1
2	3.1	1.4	2.0	1.4
3	3.6	2.8	3.7	2.8
4	3.9	3.7	5.8	3.7
5	4.5	4.5	6.0	4.5
6	5.5	5.5	7.5	6.5
7	6.0	8.0	8.0	8.5
8	8.0	10.0	12.0	11.0
9	13.0	15.0	15.5	17.0
10	51.0	48.0	38.0	43.5
Gini coefficient	0.55	0.57	0.49	0.57

Source: Urrutia and Berry, *La Distribucion del Ingreso en Colombia;* and DANE (EH-4).

Table 40. *Income Distribution from Labor Force Surveys, 1971 and 1978*
(accumulated percent)

EH-3, April 1971		EH-5, November 1971		EH-19, April 1978[a]	
Employed population	*Income*	*Employed population*	*Income*	*Employed population*	*Income*
36.6	7.0	36.9	7.5	—	—
66.0	23.9	65.7	24.9	20	4.8
80.3	37.6	79.0	38.3	40	15.0
90.8	52.9	90.8	53.0	50	21.4
100.0	100.0	100.0	100.0	60	28.8
				80	46.3
				90	60.9
				100	100.0

—Data not available.

a. DANE did not publish the results of EH-19. The Corporacion Centro Regional de Poblacion tabulated this income distribution for Fedesarrollo, plus distributions by household and household income per capita for urban and rural areas as well as for Bogota and the whole nation.

Source: DANE.

EH-3 (April 1971) and EH-5 (November 1971) are labor force surveys similar to EH-19. Table 40 shows that in the first two surveys, the top three deciles of the distribution have a similar share of total income.

Table 40 compares the three distributions and suggests that income concentration decreased between 1971 and 1978. The lowest four income deciles seem to have improved their participation in the national income as was suggested in the study of the rich and the poor in Cali. The participation of the upper 10 percent of the population, on the contrary, decreased according to the surveys. Because the 1978 survey appears to cover a greater proportion of the national income, one would expect the participation of the tenth decile to be higher in 1978 than in 1971, if one assumes that underestimation is higher in the upper deciles.[13] On the contrary, the degree of underestimation in general decreased from 1971 to 1978; therefore, the decrease in participation of the top two deciles strongly supports the hypothesis that income distribution improved in this period.

Another possible comparison is between the Selowsky survey of 1974 and the 1978 distribution. Table 41 shows this comparison. Once again, the data are not really comparable, but, nevertheless, they indicate that income distribution has improved. Between 1970 and 1974, urban industrial wages deteriorated; therefore, the urban income distributions shown in Table 41 for the early 1970s show no improvement. In the second part of the decade, when real industrial wages improved, the urban distribution also improved.

Even though the household surveys point to an improvement in the income distribution during the 1970s, their large underestimation of rural incomes casts some doubt on their overall reliability. This suggests that one should focus attention solely on the results of the surveys for the urban areas. Table 42, which displays the urban income distributions in EH-4 and EH-19, once again suggests an improvement: the income of the top urban quintile decreased from 60 percent to 53.7 percent in 1978, while that of the bottom two quintiles increased from 9 percent in 1971 to 15 percent of total income. The participation of the fourth quintile, which represents the middle class, decreased from 19.5 percent to 17.5 percent. Table 42, therefore, is consistent with the findings reported in Chapters 2 and 3 on the basis of quite different sources of data.

One last survey—EH-21, a joint DANE and World Bank survey of December 1978—offers further evidence of an improvement in the urban income distribution during the decade. This survey of the income distribution for Bogota is of very high quality and quite comparable with EH-4 (1971). Table 43 compares the data for Bogota in these two surveys

Table 41. Gini Coefficients for Various Income Distributions, 1964–78

Distribution	Urban	Rural	Total
Urrutia-Berry (1964)[a]	0.48	0.55	0.57
DANE EH-4 (1971)[a]	0.54	0.49	0.57
Sandoval-Urrutia (1972)[a]	0.54	0.62	0.58
Selowsky (1974)[b]	0.54	0.42	0.50
DANE EH-19 (1978)[c]	0.45	0.44	0.47

a. Distribution of income among economically active persons.
b. Distribution of income among households.
c. Distribution of income among employed persons.
Source: Tables 33, 34, 35, 36, 37, and 39.

Table 42. Urban Income Distribution by Quintiles of Family Income per Capita, 1971 and 1978
(percent of total income)

Quintiles of family income per capita	EH-4 1971	EH-19 1978
1	2.5	4.8
2	6.5	10.2
3	11.0	13.8
4	19.5	17.5
5	60.0	53.7

Source: DANE.

Table 43. Income Distribution among Income Earners in Bogota, 1971–78
(percent of total income in decile)

Decile of the economically active population	EH-4 1971	EH-19 April 1978	EH-21 December 1978
1	1.6	1.8	2.74
2	1.5	3.5	3.42
3	2.4	4.4	3.73
4	3.0	5.0	4.21
5	4.0	5.5	5.14
6	6.0	6.6	6.20
7	8.5	7.6	7.76
8	12.0	9.6	11.21
9	18.0	14.6	17.61
10	44.0	41.4	37.98

Source: DANE.

and shows a considerable improvement in income distribution. Again, the first five deciles increase their participation, and both the middle class and the upper class (tenth decile) register relative losses. A 1980 study by Mohan, Garcia, and Wagner estimates that EH-21 covers as much as 86.4 percent of income generated in Bogota.[14] Therefore, the income distribution for December 1978, because of its high level of coverage, should have a high income participation of the upper deciles, because high income coverage in a survey usually implies little underestimation of high incomes. For that reason, the improvement in income distribution shown in Table 43 cannot be ascribed to changes in the quality of the survey data.

In summary, the data from all sources point to an improvement in the income distribution between 1971 and 1978.

Conclusion

Comparing income distributions derived from different household surveys is always risky because of differences in coverage and in the quality of the income data. Nevertheless, an analysis of several such distributions carefully controlled in terms of similar data and similar methodologies does not support the common belief that income has become more concentrated in Colombia in the last fifteen years. On the contrary, the distribution remained constant in the 1960s and improved in the 1970s.

Many phenomena contributed to this result. Unquestionably, the improvement in the income of rural laborers and small farmers avoided the deterioration of the distribution in the 1960s and helped to diminish income dispersion in the 1970s. Also, government policy in the 1970s consciously attempted to improve distribution. Interestingly, the greatest opposition to the development model adopted by the government in the 1970s came from the employer federations, which were also the groups that promoted the belief that income concentration increased in the decade.

Finally, the household survey data are consistent with the wage series by occupation analyzed in Chapter 2 and the analysis of family incomes in Cali described in Chapter 3. All the evidence suggests that the middle class did well in the 1960s and lost ground in the 1970s and that the poorest families improved their standards of living, particularly in the latter half of the 1970s.

Notes to Chapter 4

1. These were EH-2 (1970), which was never published; EH-4 (1971); and EH-6 (1972).
2. Only EH-1 (1970), EH-3 (1971), EH-5 (1971), and EH-19 (1978) were national surveys, and

only these have rural information. The other surveys have covered four cities in some cases and seven cities in others.

3. See Marcelo Selowsky, *Who Benefits from Government Expenditure? A Case Study of Colombia* (New York: Oxford University Press, 1979); and Ulpiano Ayala and Nohra Rey de Marulanda, *Empleo y Pobreza* (Bogota: CEDE, Universidad de los Andes, July 1978).

4. This was the 1972 Oficina de Planeacion del Sector Agropecuario (OPSA)–United States Agency for International Development (USAID), *Muestra de Ampliacion* of the 1970 agricultural census.

5. Albert Berry and Alfonso Padilla, "La Distribucion de Ingresos Provenientes de la Agricultura en Colombia—1960," Universidad Nacional, Documento de Trabajo (Bogota: CID, January/March 1970).

6. Miguel Urrutia and Albert Berry, *La Distribucion del Ingreso en Colombia* (Medellin: Editorial la Carreta, 1975).

7. This involved calculating the income of rural artisans in each department and assigning incomes to the other nonagricultural rural workers who appeared in the 1964 population census. These incomes were derived from a rural survey found in Rafael Prieto, Bill Hanneson, and Marco Reyes, *Estudio Agronomico de la Hoya del Rio Suarez* (Bogota: CEDE, 1965).

8. Rafael Isaza and Francisco Ortega, *Ensuestas Urbanas de Empleo y Desempleo* (Bogota: CEDE, 1968).

9. The Gini coefficient measures the degree of concentration of an income distribution. The coefficient is 1 when all income is controlled by one person, and 0 when everyone has the same income. For a simple explanation of the Gini coefficient, see Urrutia and Berry, *La Distribucion*, pp. 53–55.

10. Rafael Prieto and others, *Fuentes y Usos de Recursos Financieros en el Sector Agropecuario de Colombia* (Bogota: Banco de la Republica, 1976).

11. For 1972, the same agricultural wage series as that used by Berry in 1960 was utilized. Therefore, the possible upward bias that would result from using the new agricultural wage series does not arise.

12. For details of how this rural income distribution for 1972 was calculated, see Clara Elsa de Sandoval and Miguel Urrutia, "Distribucion del Ingreso Proveniente de la Actividad Agropecuaria en Colombia" (Bogota: Fedesarrollo, November 1980; processed). The distribution probably overestimates the concentration of rural incomes because of an overrepresentation of large farms. This problem probably explains why the methodology produces an estimate of rural income 10 percent higher than that obtained from national income data.

13. Table 31 shows that EH-19 accounts for 56 percent of rural income, while EH-3 and EH-5 account for 36 and 40 percent of rural income. The earlier surveys therefore underestimate income to a greater extent.

14. Rakesh Mohan, M. W. Wagner, and Jorge Garcia, *Measuring Urban Malnutrition and Poverty: A Case Study of Bogota and Cali, Colombia*, World Bank Staff Working Paper no. 447 (Washington, D.C., 1981).

5

Changes in Colombia's
Urban Poverty

OVER THE YEARS, there has been a gradual decrease in rural poverty in Colombia. The real wages of rural laborers have increased, and there has been some real gain in the incomes of the rural poor between 1964 and 1972. Yet, Colombia is fast becoming an urban nation.[1] Therefore, it is important to determine what has happened to the urban poor in the recent past because, in the future, urban poverty could be a more serious problem than rural poverty.

Although the growth of the Colombian economy has been characterized as satisfactory, it has not been particularly impressive; thus, any worsening of the income distribution could possibly mean increases in the absolute levels of urban poverty.[2] In countries with much more rapid growth, such as Brazil in the 1960s, a worsening of income distribution is less likely to increase poverty levels.

Although real per capita income rose by 23.1 percent between 1958 and 1968 and by 58.3 percent between 1968 and 1978, an acceleration of inflation between 1970 and 1974 seems to have led to decreases in real urban wages. This phenomenon has led many observers in Colombia to postulate that poverty increased in the 1970s. This chapter attempts to identify the urban poor and to ascertain the extent to which urban poverty has increased or decreased.

Earlier Studies on Poverty Levels

Any study of poverty comprises several stages. The first is to define the poor. One approach is to define poor families as those whose level of welfare does not meet a set of absolute standards established more or less

93

arbitrarily. Another approach is to consider poor families as those whose welfare does not meet a set of relative conditions, also established arbitrarily, in the context of the population analyzed.

Absolute standards are usually established on the basis of family expenditures on food. This is so because specifying nutritional standards is easier than specifying minimum standards for housing and clothing, not to mention those for other components of expenditure whose behavior is less stable and systematic.

Table 44 shows various standards proposed in terms of expenditures for food, expressed in 1978 Colombian pesos. The differences are quite large: the highest estimate is five times greater than the lowest. To frame these standards within the context of the Colombian economy, it is useful to compare them with data on average income, average food expenditure, and the minimum wage. This is done in columns 2, 3, and 4 of the table, where the proposed standards are divided by the indicators just mentioned. These results will be used to determine the absolute standard that will serve as the basis for analyzing the characteristics and trends of urban poverty.

Relative standards of poverty are no less arbitrary because they can hardly be based on assessments of basic needs, which are usually specified in absolute terms. The degree of arbitrariness is reflected in the wide range of income-distribution percentiles within which various proposed standards fall. In some academic studies, for example, only the first two deciles are identified as the poor. The development plan "Para Cerrar la Brecha" and the report *Hacia el Pleno Empleo* by the International Labour Organisation (ILO) propose that economic policy should favor the first five deciles.[3] In the 1984 study by Mohan and Hartline, the poor are those making up the first three deciles.[4] The income distribution for 1964 indicates that those at the upper limit of the fifth decile have an income approximately four times greater than those at the upper limit of the first decile. This ambiguity naturally reflects the fact that poverty is not a binary variable but rather a problem of degree.

Previous studies have offered various estimates of absolute poverty, which is usually expressed as the percentage of persons living below an arbitrary poverty line. Using criterion A of Table 44, Bourguignon found that 59 percent of Colombian families were poor in 1974.[5] Applying alternative C, Altimir calculated that 38 percent of urban families and 54 percent of rural families were poor in 1970; this gave a national average of 45 percent.[6] According to Mohan and Hartline, alternative D would place 30 percent of the families of Bogota below the poverty line in 1977.[7] These findings obviously are not comparable because they are based on different estimates of minimum food expenditures.

Table 44. *Alternative Standards Proposed for Minimum Monthly Food Expenditure per Adult Person*
(1978 Colombian pesos)

Alternative	Normative monthly food expenditure (1978 Colombian pesos) (1)	Proportion of average income (2)	Proportion of average food expenditure (3)	Proportion of minimum wage (4)
A	1,705	0.72	2.36	0.66
B	822	0.35	1.14	0.32
C	696	0.29	0.96	0.27
D	535	0.22	0.74	0.21
E	341	0.14	0.47	0.13

Source: For column 1: Alternative A is taken from DANE (1973). Alternative B is taken from tabulation prepared by Aquiles Arellano for a study on family poverty using figures from the Family Budget Survey conducted by the Centro de Estudios para el Desarrollo Economico (CEDE) of the Universidad de los Andes in 1967–1968. Alternative C is the estimate given in Oscar Altimir, *The Extent of Poverty in Latin America: A Summary* (Santiago, 1978; processed), p. 24. According to that estimate, the annual minimum diet would have cost US$85 in 1970. This figure was converted to pesos by taking the average buying quotation for the exchange certificate in that year (Col$18.45). Alternative D was calculated by Jorge Garcia, and also is mentioned in Rakesh Mohan and Nancy Hartline, *The Poor of Bogota: Who They Are, What They Earn, Where They Live*, World Bank Staff Working Paper no. 635 (Washington, D.C., 1984), p. 6. Alternative E results from a calculation of the minimum food expenditure that would purchase a basket that meets the nutritional standards of the Instituto Colombiana de Bienestar Familiar. The calculation gives weight to the original estimates for the seven cities (Bogota, Cali, Barranquilla, Medellin, Bucaramanga, Pasto, and Manizales) according to population. All figures have been converted to 1978 Colombian pesos in accordance with the food price index prepared by DANE for the blue-collar consumer.

For column 2: This column shows the arithmetic ratio of the minimum expenditure estimates of column 1 to monthly per capita income in 1978. The latter was obtained by dividing total national income for 1978, as shown in the Banco de la Republic national accounts, by the population estimate given in U.S. Department of Commerce (1979), table 1, page 5, for 1978 (25,673,000). (For full details, see Mauricio Carrizosa, "Determinantes de las Ingresos y la Pobreza en Colombia" [Bogota: CEDE, 1981; processed.]) The monthly per capita income thus calculated is Col$2,379.

For column 3: This column shows the arithmetic ratio of the minimum expenditure estimates of column 1 to estimated average monthly expenditure for food (Col$722). To obtain the latter, the proportion of food expenditure in household consumption was calculated first by using the input-output matrix for 1976 prepared by DANE. This proportion was 36.8 percent and was multiplied by "private consumption expenditure" for 1978, given in Banco de la Republica national accounts, to obtain estimated total food expenditure. Per capita expenditure is based on the population estimates for 1978 mentioned in the preceding note.

For column 4: In this column, the estimates of minimum food expenditure are divided by the monthly minimum wage. The daily minimum wage in effect in May 1978 (Col$86) was multiplied by thirty days to obtain the monthly figure of Col$2,580.

No studies attempt to measure relative poverty in Colombia. Some investigations of inequality, however, do provide relative quantitative indicators that can be used to analyze the problem of relative poverty. Specifically, as shown by Sen, the Gini coefficient is a special case of the measure of poverty.[8] The Sen measure of poverty P can be expressed as follows:

$$P = H [I + (1 - I) G]$$

where H is the percentage of the population considered poor, I is the average gap between the normative income and the income of the poor expressed as a percentage of the normative income, and G is the Gini coefficient for the population studied. If the entire population is included in P (that is, $H = 1$) and per capita income is taken as the norm, then $I = 0$ and consequently $P = G$. The terms of reference of this special case of Sen's measure—namely, consideration of the total population and the adoption of average income as the norm—clearly implies that it must be interpreted as a measure of relative poverty.

If the foregoing interpretation is accepted, studies that estimate the Gini coefficient could be used to determine what has happened to relative urban poverty over time. Unfortunately, the available studies do not make possible any comparison of the Gini coefficient of family income per capita or that of income per equivalent consumer through time. These measures would be the most useful ones for our purposes. Table 34 in Chapter 4, however, includes various Gini coefficients for comparable distributions of income earners. These coefficients suggest a constant level of relative poverty between 1964 and 1972 and a decrease in relative poverty in the 1970s.

Finally, it is useful to summarize the available findings on the characteristics of poverty. In two recent studies, Musgrove and Ferber analyze the problem of identifying the poor.[9] Some of their findings are useful for the analysis developed below.

• Poverty can be identified on the basis of income from work, because poor families receive no significant income from other sources. This finding is important because the published tabulations of the DANE labor force surveys distribute employed persons according to income from work. Consequently, using these distributions to identify the employed poor and also to compare absolute poverty eliminates the risk of major error.

• Educational level is the classifying variable that best distinguishes households by income level. This finding will help in the use of tabulations that combine educational level with other variables to identify which of these other variables can be associated with poverty.

• In the Colombian cities (Bogota and Medellin) studied, the sectors of construction and domestic service show high percentages of poverty. This finding suggests that the movement of average income of these poor groups should be analyzed.

Some argue that our knowledge of poverty would be more complete if the analysis took into account the supposed segmentation in labor markets—between the formal and informal sectors, the modern and nonmodern sectors, the marginal and traditional sectors, and so on. Two studies of the Colombian case show no results that would confirm the validity of such distinctions in the 1970s. Kugler, Reyes, and Gomez state:

> When we control for sex, education, and experience, the difference in average income from work [among sectors] disappears. In general, no significant differences are observed. Not even the fact that the modern sector offers its employees fringe benefits more frequently than the nonmodern sector seems to affect differentially the average incomes of persons with identical levels of education and experience.[10]

Bourguignon's 1979 study of Bogota yields a similar result:

> When the most common determinants of income are used correctly the income differential between the modern and traditional sectors decreases greater. It falls from approximately 100% to 20%, and on average, the lower limit in the confidence interval of 95% for that differential does not exceed 10%.[11]

The distinction between traditional and modern is often used to identify poverty groups. The studies mentioned, however, do not support the use of these classifications to identify trends in poverty. Even if relatively poor persons are found in the informal, marginal, or nonmodern sectors, that fact is not very useful for analyzing changes in the incomes of the poor since these categories usually are not presented in income tabulations. In any event, the studies mentioned suggest that it is not worth the effort in Colombia to try to classify the population according to modern and traditional sectors to study poverty trends.

Mohan's 1980 paper gives a rather complete characterization of the poor in Bogota, based on the DANE surveys EH-8 (March 1975) and EH-15 (June 1977).[12] The results, some of them surprising, are summarized and discussed below:

• Among poor households, the largest ones are relatively less poor. Mohan finds, however, that the number of household members per worker is constant beginning with a family size of five. Actually, as Carrizosa shows, the critical variable of the family structure for purposes of an analysis of poverty is the number of employed persons per household member.[13]

• Persons without education are probably poor at any age. Those with primary education also are likely to be poor, but the probability of poverty is greater for those under fourteen years of age, between thirty-five and forty-four, and over sixty-five. In this analysis, we distinguish these two educational categories to identify some other characteristics of poverty.

• Migrants are not particularly poor when compared with nonmigrants. The majority of the poor are persons who have been in Bogota more than ten years. Thus, it is inappropriate to state that migrants are the poor; a more reasonable hypothesis is that migration has a depressing effect on urban wages.

• The rate of unemployment is inversely related to income level. This finding can be expected to the extent that the unemployed tend to receive less income. In this analysis, we calculate rates of unemployment by educational level; the result is that the pattern of unemployment based on permanent income appears to be somewhat different. (It is assumed that education is a proxy for permanent income, and, therefore, unemployment is not as clearly inversely related to education as one would expect.)

• The rate of participation—that is, the economically active population divided by the total population over five years of age—is directly related to the income level.

• The index of concentration of poverty by occupation shows an overrepresentation of poverty among workers in services, manufacturing, construction (males), and trade (females).

• Poor males tend to work more hours a week than rich males; the opposite is true of females.

• Poverty is high in the manufacturing, construction, retail trade, transportation and communications, and personal and domestic services (males) sectors.

• At all educational levels, unemployment among the poor is greater than among those who are not poor.

The methodology used to reach this last conclusion presents a problem. By definition, an unemployed person receives less income; he certainly does not receive income from work. As a result, he tends to be included among the "poor," so that, on this basis alone, the poor would show higher rates of unemployment than those who are not poor. When Mohan classifies persons by educational level alone, however, no systematic relationship is observed between educational level and rate of unemployment. The 1977 EH-15 survey shows higher than average unemployment rates for the more educated females. Through the high school level, it also shows higher than average rates for the more educated males, whereas university graduates have an unemployment rate virtually equal to that observed for persons without education. A 1975 survey also found greater unemployment among the more educated females, except that high school graduates had a higher rate than university graduates. In the case of males, the relationship between educational level and unemployment rates is inverse. On the assumption that education is a variable that better classifies permanent income, the relationship between poverty and unemployment is not obvious.[14] We shall examine this point in greater detail in the section that follows.

Several characteristics of the poor warrant attention. There is the relationship between education and poverty. Earlier studies on income functions and on the characteristics of the poor show the expected inverse relationship between poverty and education. Taking into account that with time there may be a decrease in the returns from education, one can investigate the extent to which education contributes to the eradication of poverty.[15] Another characteristic is the age-poverty profile, which can be used to determine whether poverty is a permanent state or a transitory condition. Mohan's 1980 study and other studies on income profiles by age suggest that poverty may be a permanent condition for those affected. In the present study, we offer some additional evidence on this aspect. In addition, there is a fairly general agreement that poverty should be analyzed in a family context. For this reason, we complement our analysis of the distribution of employed persons with some evidence on family income per member.

Urban Poverty

The quantification of poverty presented here refers to different aspects of the urban sector. In general, the study is based on the data of Bogota alone; of the four largest cities (Bogota, Cali, Medellin, and Barranquilla); of three medium-size or small cities (Bucaramanga, Manizales, and Pasto); and of the urban sector as a whole. The study of Bogota alone contains the most data, with annual observations beginning in 1970 as well as some information dating back to the 1960s. For the group of the four largest cities, relatively good statistical information is available, which permits calculations on poverty. For the three medium-size or small cities, evidence is available only for the period 1973–80. Finally, indicators have been constructed for the urban sector as a whole for individual years over a fairly long period (1964–78).

Table 45. Employed Poor in the City of Bogota, 1965–80

Year	Reference period	Survey	Price index (1)	Normative monthly income (2)	Percentage of poor (3)	Rate of participation (4)	Rate of open unemployment (5)
1965	September	CEDE	79.3	383	13.7[a]	—	15.3
1967	Full year	CEDE-PRESFAM	100.0	500	17.1[a]	—	—
1970	June	DANE EH-1	127.9	640	28.6	35.7	11.9
1971	July	DANE EH-4	136.2	681	35.5	33.3	9.4
1973	October	DANE CENSO	194.7	974	45.2[a]	—	—
1974	June	DANE EH-7	236.3	1,182	41.5	—	9.5
1975	March	DANE EH-BE	293.8	1,469	46.4	—	8.2
1976	June	DANE EH-11	345.2	1,726	41.9	36.4	6.5
1977	June	DANE EH-15	483.6	2,418	40.7	37.2	6.1
1978	September	DANE EH-20	536.8	2,684	29.3	35.8	5.1
1979	June	DANE EH-23	664.2	3,321	27.1	37.0	4.4
1980	March	DANE EH-26	781.6	3,908	19.7	38.8	6.0

—Data not available.

a. Unreliable data.

Source: For column 1: Price index is the blue-collar index for Bogota prepared by DANE, *Revista del Banco de la Republica*, various issues. The base year 1967 = 100.

For column 2: Normative monthly income: see text.

For column 3: Within each distribution of employed persons, the number situated in the interval below norm was aggregated. To this sum was added a proportion of the interval that includes the value of the poverty norm.

For column 4: Rate of participation is the economically active population with primary education or without education, divided by population over five years of age with primary education or without education.

For column 5: Rate of unemployment is unemployed persons with primary education or without education divided by employed persons with primary education or without education. For 1965, the figure used is the average of the rates for that year in the construction branch, reported by Rafael Isaza, "Ocupacion y Desocupacion en Bogota," *Empleo y Desempleo en Colombia* (Bogota: CEDE, Universidad de los Andes, 1968).

For 1965: Richard Nelson, T. Paul Schultz, and Robert L. Slighton, *Structural Change in a Developing Economy; Colombia's Problems and Prospects* (Princeton, N.J.: Princeton University Press, 1971), p. 146. Primary source is unpublished data of CEDE, Universidad de los Andes.

For 1967: Rafael Prieto, "Gasto e Ingreso Familiar Urbano en Colombia," *Ensayos ECIEL*, no. 4 (August 1977), p. 115. This is a family distribution. To make it comparable with the distribution of employed persons, the norm of Col$500 was adjusted to Col$1,000, because each family has an average of two employed persons. This assumption is based on the fact that the rate of participation of uneducated persons is nearly 0.35, and average family size is six to seven persons.

For 1970–80: DANE.

101

The first results presented are those for the percentage of the poor in the population. A poverty line of about Col$500 a month per employed person was selected for them in 1967. This is equivalent to Col$2,780 in 1978 pesos. The highest alternative for the normative food expenditure shown in Table 44 represents 61 percent of this amount; this figure is approximately equal to the minimum wage established in May 1978. In selecting this figure, the upper limit of the lowest income bracket in the tabulations of the DANE surveys (Col$500 a month in 1970) was taken into account. The resulting standard would be too high for the analysis of per capita family income. Nonetheless, it seems reasonable to use this upper limit in the analysis of the incomes of economically active people because employed persons have dependents to support.[16] It can also be used to make comparisons over time, which probably do not depend significantly on the absolute standard adopted.

The results for Bogota are shown in Table 45. By limiting the analysis to that city, it is possible to estimate a series for a fifteen-year period from 1965. As seen in the table, information was available for nearly all years of the 1970s and for two years of the preceding decade. To express normative income in current-year pesos for the corresponding reference period, the blue-collar consumer price index was used for the city of Bogota. To aid in interpreting the figure for the percentage of poor, the last two columns of the table show the rates of participation and of unemployment for persons without education or with primary education. According to the series obtained, the percentage of poor seems to increase from 1965 to 1975 and then decline until March 1980, the latest date for which information is available.

As was mentioned in Chapter 4, the census income data for 1973 are very unreliable, and underestimation of incomes is substantial. The absolute levels of poverty are therefore clearly overestimated in 1973 in the table.

The income figures for 1965 and 1967, in contrast, seem suspiciously high. The CEDE-PRESFAM income data give higher average incomes than those obtained in the other surveys. In 1968 constant pesos, the 1967 PRESFAM average income is Col$25,024 a year, whereas the EH-4 (1971) survey has only Col$21,498 a year after four years of high per capita income growth at the national level. The PRESFAM data also give a better income distribution than other sources. For all these reasons, this 1967 data source is not comparable with other income sources, although in fact this survey may have income data of good quality. Also, the PRESFAM survey is not a random sample, and the assumptions used to derive the distribution from a stratified sample may create serious biases. In summary, the poverty trends

Table 46. *Rate of Participation in Bogota, 1970–80*

			Rate of participation (percent)	
Year	Reference period	Survey	Total population	Population without education or with primary education
1970	June	DANE EH-1	54.5	35.7
1971	July	DANE EH-4	49.3	33.3
1972	September	DANE EH-6	46.2	—
1973	October	DANE CENSO	46.1	—
1974	June	DANE EH-7	51.9	—
1975	March	DANE EH-8E	50.3	—
1976	June	DANE EH-11	51.0	36.4
1977	June	DANE EH-15	49.8	37.2
1978	September	DANE EH-20	50.5	35.8
1979	June	DANE EH-23	51.6	37.0
1980	March	DANE EH-26	56.4	38.8

—Data not available.
Source: The total rate of participation is taken from DANE, *Boletin Mensual de Estadistica* no. 345 (1980), pp. 71 and 74. The rate of participation of the population without education or with primary education is taken from Table 45. The level of the two rates is not wholly comparable because the first covers the population over ten years of age, whereas the second covers the population over five years of age.

of the 1960s may be a result of changes in the quality of the data and may not reflect changes in real poverty levels.

It is also probably misleading to compare the EH-1 1970 survey with other income surveys. The 1970 survey was probably the best and the most thorough of these surveys, and it appears to have much less income underestimation.

A basic limitation of the foregoing exercise is that income distributions for employed persons have been used. It is possible that the observed increase in the proportion of poor people in some years simply reflects a trend toward more participation in the labor force by members of poor families. Table 46 shows the rate of labor force participation in Bogota for the total population and for the population over five years of age without education or with primary education. Actually, the rate of participation of the total population declined somewhat between 1970 and 1979, while the percentage of the poor employed was rising. Consequently, at least part of the increase in the percentage of employed persons living below the poverty line could be attributed to a greater relative participation in the labor force by persons with a low level of education. This and other problems of interpretation can be attributed to the fact that distributions of employed persons are not the most suitable measure of family welfare.

Another problem with calculating changes in the degree of poverty on the basis of the income of the employed is that this leaves out the problem of unemployment, and one positive aspect of the period analyzed is the behavior of the unemployment rate, which decreased significantly. This trend is shown in Table 47 for the total economically active population and for the group with no education or with only primary education. Table 48 adds the uneducated unemployed to the poor; it therefore shows the percentage of the economically active population that is below the poverty line. It can be seen that the inclusion of unemployed persons does not substantially change the poverty trends shown in Table 45 for Bogota.

The unemployment series presented in Table 47 reveals one change: the unemployment rate for uneducated persons is higher than the average rate in 1963–67 and lower in the 1970s. On the average, unemployment of uneducated persons in 1963–66 was 11 percent, while the overall rate was 8.7 percent. The average figures for 1977–80 were 5.4 percent for the uneducated and 7.5 percent overall.

The change in the pattern of unemployment can be seen better in Table 49, which shows the coefficient of concentration of employed persons without any education or with only primary education in Bogota. This coefficient is defined as the ratio of the proportion of unemployed persons without education or with primary education in the total number of unemployed to the proportion of the labor force without education or with primary education in the total labor force. It is a measure of the "overrepresentation" of unemployment of the poor. As shown in the table, throughout the 1970s, unemployed persons without education or with primary education got progressively more underrepresented. In other words, their participation in unemployment was progressively less than their participation in the labor force. The change probably occurred at the end of the 1960s. The corresponding index of concentration for blue-collar workers and nonfarm production workers was 1.64 for 1963, 1.49 for 1964, 1.48 for 1965, 0.85 for 1974, and 0.97 for 1978.[17] In other words, it appears that during the 1960s unemployment was concentrated among the poorest groups, whereas during the 1970s the poor represented a comparatively smaller proportion of the unemployed.

Table 48 indicates a sharp decline in the percentage of the poor after 1977, with the percentage in 1980 being significantly lower than that observed at the beginning of the 1970s. Correspondingly, data on the incomes of unskilled workers indicate that poverty was less extensive in 1978–80 than during the 1960s. Those incomes rose considerably in the

Table 47. *Rate of Unemployment in Bogota, 1963–80*

			Rate of unemployment	
Year	Reference period	Survey	Overall	Employed persons without education or with primary education
1963	June	CEDE	8.7	9.4
1964	June	CEDE	7.2	11.6
1965	June	CEDE	8.8	13.0
1966	March	CEDE	10.1	12.9
1967	June	CEDE	12.7	—
1970	June	DANE EH-1	13.1	11.9
1971	July	DANE EH-4	9.2	9.4
1972	September	DANE EH-6	7.4	—
1973	October	DANE CENSO	10.7	—
1974	June	DANE EH-7	11.1	9.5
1975	March	DANE EH-8E	10.2	8.2
1976	June	DANE EH-11	8.4	6.5
1977	June	DANE EH-15	7.8	6.1
1978	September	DANE EH-20	6.7	5.1
1979	June	DANE EH-23	6.1	4.4
1980	March	DANE EH-26	9.5	6.0

—Data not available.
Source: The overall unemployment rate is taken from DANE, *Boletin Mensual de Estadistica* no. 345 (1980), pp. 83, 86. The unemployment rate for uneducated persons or those with primary education is taken from Table 45. For 1963–67, the unemployment rate of uneducated persons is based on employment, in the construction sector as reported in Rafael Isaza, "Ocupacion y Desocupacion en Bogota," *Empleo y Desempleo en Colombia* (Bogota: CEDE, Universidad de los Andes, 1968).

Table 48. *Percentage of Poor in the Economically Active Population of Bogota, 1970–80*

Year	Reference period	Survey	Percentage of poor
1970	June	DANE EH-1	31.4
1971	July	DANE EH-2	37.7
1974	June	DANE EH-7	44.9
1975	March	DANE EH-8E	45.8
1976	June	DANE EH-11	41.4
1977	June	DANE EH-15	40.4
1978	September	DANE EH-20	29.5
1979	June	DANE EH-23	27.4
1980	March	DANE EH-26	20.0

Source: Unemployed persons without education or with primary education were added to the employed "poor" and the resulting figure was divided by the total economically active population. The primary data sources are indicated in Table 44.

Table 49. *Coefficient of Concentration of Unemployed Persons without Education or with Primary Education in Bogota, 1970–80*

Year	Reference period	Survey	Index of concentration[a]
1970	June	DANE EH-1	0.91
1971	July	DANE EH-4	1.03
1974	June	DANE EH-7	0.86
1977	June	DANE EH-15	0.78
1980	March	DANE EH-26	0.63

a. The index of concentration is $1 = di/fi$, where di is unemployed persons without education or with primary education as a percentage of total unemployment, and fi is the economically active population without education or with primary education as a percentage of the total economically active population.

Source: DANE.

Table 50. *Real Monthly Incomes of Selected Low-Income Groups in Bogota, 1976–80*
(constant 1976 Colombian pesos)

Year	Reference period	Survey	Service workers	Nonfarm laborers and production workers	Construction workers
1976	June	EH-11	316	545	489
1980	March	EH-26	441	676	694

Source: DANE. Real incomes are arrived at by using the blue-collar consumer price index.

late 1970s, exceeding the maximum levels reached in earlier years. The same cannot be said about the incomes of skilled blue-collar workers (those working in manufacturing, for instance); for these, the recovery in real wages in the late 1970s was not sufficient to regain the levels reached earlier in the decade. But these workers clearly cannot be included among the poor.

Table 50 presents additional evidence on the incomes of the poor. As Musgrove and Ferber (1978 and 1979) and Mohan and Hartline (1984) have shown, service workers and nonfarm laborers, as well as construction workers, have comparatively high indexes of poverty. Average incomes have been calculated for these groups in Bogota for 1976 and 1980. Although the differences in the quality of the data make it difficult to compare absolute income levels, real incomes do appear to have improved.

The consistency of the data from labor force surveys can be analyzed by using the Bogota data. One way of doing this is to compare the "most frequent income" bracket shown in the surveys for construction workers with the nominal monthly wage reported to DANE by construction firms. It can be reasonably assumed that the most common worker in the construction sector is the unskilled laborer. Table 51 presents such a comparison and, in general, the two sets of statistics are similar. It can be concluded, therefore, that for this income level the survey data are accurate.

The study of the survey data for the four largest cities together complements the analysis made for Bogota. Table 52 shows the high percentage of the poor observed in 1974–77 and the subsequent decline in this indicator. It also shows the decrease in unemployment that occurred during the decade as well as the increase in the rate of participation.

Table 53 presents the degrees of poverty for three small- or medium-size cities (Bucaramanga, Manizales, and Pasto). The trend for the proportion of the poor is similar to that observed for the four largest cities, although the percentage is higher. This is explained largely by the structure of the economically active population by educational level. In the four largest cities, the proportion of persons without education or with primary education in the total labor force is 0.46 percent; the corresponding figure for Bucaramanga, Manizales, and Pasto is 0.51 percent. The unemployment and participation in the three cities show the same pattern noted earlier—namely, a decrease in unemployment and an increase in participation.

The results for the urban sector as a whole, which are shown in Table 54, confirm what has been said already. Poverty increased at the start of the 1970s and decreased at the end of the decade.

Another way of identifying trends in urban poverty is to examine the rates of participation and unemployment by age and educational level. Table 55 shows these rates for the urban sector as a whole. They indicate cycles of participation and employment over the life span. The poor participate in the labor force more at the beginning of the life cycle, rather than investing in education. Later, they participate relatively less as they find job opportunities that are comparatively less remunerative. Unemployment characterizes young workers regardless of educational level; later, at the usual productive ages, it affects all groups except university graduates.

As noted in the analysis of the data for Bogota, the pattern of unemployment according to educational level changed during the 1970s. At the end of the decade, not only was unemployment lower, but it was also distributed more widely within the labor force. Thus, it no longer had such a particular impact on the poor as it did during part of the 1960s.

Table 51. Most Frequent Incomes in the Construction Sector and Monthly Labor Costs for Apprentices, 1973–80
(Colombian pesos)

Year	Reference period	Survey	Modal bracket in the survey for the construction sector	Monthly income bracket according to construction costs (DANE)
1973	October	DANE-CENSO	500–1,000	742–1,012
1975	March	DANE EH-9	—	1,175–1,603
1976	June	DANE EH-11	1,000–1,500	1,372–1,870
1977	June	DANE EH-15	1,500–2,000	1,694–2,311
1978	September	DANE EH-20	2,500–3,000	2,400–3,272
1979	June	DANE EH-23	3,000–4,000	3,138–4,279
1980	March	DANE EH-26	4,000–5,000	3,914–5,337

—Data not available.

Source: These survey brackets were found to have the largest number of employed persons among the distributions of employed persons in the construction sector. The other brackets are defined as the range between what a construction apprentice would earn for twenty-two days of work per month and what he would earn for thirty days of work per month. The income of a construction apprentice was calculated on the basis of the indexes published in various issues of the DANE Boletín Mensual de Estadística, which take as the base value a daily wage of Col$25.70 in December 1971.

Table 52. *Poverty in Bogota, Cali, Medellin, and Barranquilla, 1974–80*

Year	Reference period	Survey	Price index Original base	Price index 1967	Normative monthly income	Percentage of poor	Rate of participation[a]	Rate of open unemployment
1974	June	DANE EH-7	862.4	236.7	1,184	44.4	—	11.9
1975	October	DANE EH-9	1,100.5	302.0	1,510	42.9	—	9.7
1976	June	DANE EH-11	1,261.8	346.3	1,732	43.6	35.1	9.1
1977	June	DANE EH-15	1,794.3	492.4	2,462	45.2	36.3	8.5
1978	September	DANE EH-20	2,010.4	551.7	2,758	34.0	36.2	6.5
1979	June	DANE EH-23	2,459.0	674.8	3,374	29.8	37.2	7.3
1980	March	DANE EH-26	2,883.3	791.2	3,956	21.4	38.5	8.5

—Data not available.

a. Rate of participation: economically active population with primary education or without education, divided by population over five years of age with primary education or without education.

Source: Price index: weighted average of blue-collar indexes for Bogota, Cali, Medellin, and Barranquilla prepared by DANE, *Revista del Banco de la Republica*, various issues. The weights are based on the population of each city in 1973. Normative monthly income: see text. Percentages of poor, rate of participation, and rate of unemployment: see Table 45. Income data 1974–80: DANE.

Table 53. *Percentage of Poverty in Bucaramanga, Manizales, and Pasto, 1975–80*

			Price index		Normative monthly income	Percentage of poor	Rate of participation	Rate of unemployment
Year	Reference period	Survey	Original	Base 1967				
1975	October	DANE EH-9	1,191.7	311.0	1,555	48.8	—	10.0
1976	March	DANE EH-10	1,302.5	339.9	1,700	53.4	37.0	9.0
1977	September	DANE EH-16	1,927.7	503.0	2,515	50.5	38.3	7.7
1978	September	DANE EH-20	2,171.6	566.7	2,834	40.9	36.1	6.2
1979	September	DANE EH-24	2,822.8	736.6	3,683	40.7	36.7	6.0
1980	March	DANE EH-26	3,174.7	828.5	4,142	30.9	38.5	6.3

—Data not available.

Source: Price index: weighted average of the blue-collar indexes for Bucaramanga, Manizales, and Pasto prepared by DANE, *Revista del Banco de la Republica*, various issues. The weights are based on the population of those cities in 1973. Normative monthly income: see text. Percentage of poor and rate of participation: see Table 45.

Table 54. Poverty in the Urban Sector of Colombia, 1971–78

Year	Reference period	Survey	Price index	Normative monthly income	Percentage of poor	Rate of participation	Rate of unemployment
1971	July	DANE EH-4	136.1	680	42.42	31.5	10.9
1972	September	DANE EH-6	159.9	800	47.04	—	—
1974	November	DANE EH-8	257.3	1,286	51.30	32.6	9.2
1978	June	DANE EH-19	567.8	2,839	41.95	35.1	6.5

— Data not available.

Source: Price index: total for blue-collar workers in seven cities prepared by DANE, *Revista del Banco de la República*, various issues. Normative monthly income: see text. Percentage of poor, rate of participation, and rate of unemployment: see Table 45. Distribution of employed persons: population with primary education or without education (total over five years of age, economically active, and unemployed). 1971: DANE, *Encuesta Nacional de Hogares-Fuerza de Trabajo 1971* (Bogota: July 1976). 1972: DANE, *Emensta Nacional de Hogares, 1972* (December 1977), p. 58. This is a distribution of recipients; to obtain the proportion of *employed* persons below the poverty line of Col\$800 per month, the ratio of *employed* persons to poor income recipients observed in EH-4 (1.64) was multiplied by the proportion of poor income recipients observed in EH-6. 1974–78: DANE.

Table 55. Rates of Participation and Unemployment by Age and Educational Level, 1978

Educational level	10–11	12–14	15–19	20–29	30–39	40–49	50–59	60–69	70–79
None									
Rate of participation	0.08	0.45	0.44	0.54	0.60	0.56	0.52	0.37	0.18
Rate of unemployment	0.24	0.05	0.14	0.07	0.04	0.01	0.06	0.02	0.03
Primary									
Rate of participation	0.01	0.11	0.56	0.66	0.64	0.62	0.54	0.40	0.19
Rate of unemployment	0.03	0.11	0.14	0.10	0.03	0.03	0.04	0.04	0.10
Secondary									
Rate of participation		0.03	0.22	0.68	0.70	0.68	0.56	0.39	0.26
Rate of unemployment		0.24	0.18	0.11	0.04	0.04	0.02	0.05	0.00
University									
Rate of participation			0.16	0.61	0.92	0.93	0.81	0.41	0.55
Rate of unemployment			0.43	0.12	0.01	0.00	0.00	0.00	0.00

Note: The rate of participation is defined as the economically active population in each age-educational level group, divided by the population over five years of age in that group. The rate of unemployment is defined as the ratio of unemployed persons to the economically active population in each group.
Source: The original data are from Phase 19 (June 1978) of the DANE household survey.

Table 56. *Poverty by Employment or Unemployment in the Urban Sector, 1978*

Category	Percentage of the poor in category (1)	Distribution of employment and unemployment among the poor (2)	Percentage of the total economically active population (3)	Coefficient of concentration (2 ÷ 3)
Unemployed	50.4	6.5	7.6	0.86
Employed	59.5	93.5	92.4	1.01
Total	58.8	100.0	100.0	100.0

Source: DANE, *Boletin Mensual de Estadistica* no. 326 (September 1978), pp. 39 and 57. The "poor" are defined as those who have a primary education as a maximum.

Table 56 classifies the labor force on the basis of employed and unemployed persons. The first column shows that approximately one-half of the unemployed are comparatively "poor" (persons with primary education as their highest level). The second column shows that of the total number of "poor" in the labor force, 6.5 percent are unemployed. The third column indicates that 7.6 percent of the total labor force is unemployed. In other words, unemployment among the comparatively "poor" is lower than overall unemployment. Consequently, the last column, which shows the arithmetic ratio of the second column to the third, gives an index of concentration of unemployment among the poor of slightly less than one. All of this means that unemployment is not confined to the poorest groups. It does not mean that unemployment is not a particularly serious condition for them. It obviously is, because, unlike persons in the higher income strata, the poor do not have supplementary incomes to offset the lack of income from work during periods of unemployment.

Conclusion

The study of poverty levels in this chapter depends greatly on the quality of the income data in the surveys used. As has been repeatedly explained, coverage and levels of underestimation vary among surveys. But because basic labor income is reported more accurately than other types of income, the observed changes in the percentage of wage earners below an absolute poverty line may approximate real changes in poverty levels for this group. The high concentration of poverty among the self-employed, on the other hand, may reflect more the problem of capturing this income in the surveys

Table 57. *Poverty by Occupational Level in the Urban Sector, 1974*

Occupational group	Percentage of poor at occupational level (1)	Percentage of poor accounted for by each occupation (2)	Percentage of total number of employed (3)	Coefficient of concentration (4)
White-collar workers	37.9	27.0	36.6	0.74
Blue-collar workers	62.1	25.9	21.4	1.21
Employers	18.6	1.3	3.7	0.35
Self-employed workers	57.0	28.4	25.6	1.11
Unpaid family workers	100.0	6.7	3.4	1.97
Domestic workers	97.8	17.3	9.1	1.90
Total	51.3	100.0	100.0	1.00

Note: The total of column 2 is greater than 100 because of errors in the published statistics.
Source: DANE.

than real poverty (Table 57). Therefore, the poverty trends in this section probably show the direction of change. However, small differences in the coefficients should not be considered significant.

The problem posed by the income data is well illustrated by the information from the PRESFAM 1967 survey. This is probably the most carefully done of all the surveys, and it shows both less poverty and a better income distribution.[18] Although the sample may have underrepresented the poor, it is very probable that careful questions concerning the income of the poor eliminates substantial underreporting of the income of the self-employed.

But if we ignore problems of levels and concentrate on trends derived from the data of similar dubious quality, we get a picture of growing urban poverty from 1970 to 1975 and decreasing poverty in the second part of the decade. This picture coincides with the data on Cali at the microeconomic level presented in Chapter 3 and the data on real wages by occupational group.

A 1981 study on nutrition levels by Mohan, Wagner, and Garcia offers some additional corroborating evidence. It concludes from comparable household survey data that malnutrition in Bogota and Cali decreased from about 30 percent to 15 percent of the population between 1973 and 1978.[19]

From this analysis, it does appear that urban poverty decreased in the 1970s. It is clear, however, that in the first part of the decade, poverty increased temporarily. In the following chapter, some hypotheses will be suggested to explain the trends in poverty and income distribution shown by the data analyzed up to now.

Notes to Chapter 5

1. At the time of the 1964 census, 52.1 percent of the population lived in municipal capitals, while at the time of the 1973 census, the figure was already 63.1 percent.

2. Gustav Ranis, "Distribucion del Ingreso y Crecimiento en Colombia," *Desarrollo y Sociedad*, no. 3 (January 1980), p. 91.

3. See Departamento Nacional de Planeacion, *Para Cerrar la Brecha* (Bogota: Banco de la Republica, 1975); and International Labour Organisation (ILO), *Hacia el Pleno Empleo* (Geneva, 1970).

4. Rakesh Mohan and Nancy Hartline, *The Poor in Bogota: Who They Are, What They Earn, Where They Live*, World Bank Staff Working Paper no. 635 (Washington, D.C., 1984).

5. François Bourguignon, "Pobreza y Dualismo en el Sector Urbano de las Economias en Desarrollo: El Caso de Colombia," *Desarrollo y Sociedad* (January 1979).

6. Oscar Altimir, "The Extent of Poverty in Latin America: A Summary" (Santiago: Comicion Economica para America Latina [CEPAL], 1978; processed).

7. Mohan and Hartline, *The Poor in Bogota*.

8. Amartya Sen, "Poverty: An Ordinal Approach to Measurement," *Econometrica*, vol. 44, no. 2 (1976).

9. Philip Musgrove and Robert Ferber, "Finding the Poor," *Review of Income and Wealth*, vol. 24, no. 3 (September 1978); and Musgrove and Ferber, "Identifying the Urban Poor: Characteristics of Poverty Households in Bogota, Medellin, and Lima," *Latin American Research Review*, vol. 14, no. 2 (1979).

10. Bernardo Kugler, Alvaro Reyes, and Maria Isabel de Gomez, *Educacion y Mercado de Trabajo Urbano en Colombia: Una Comparacion entre Sectores Moderno y no Moderno*, monograph 10 (Bogota: Corporacion Centro Regional de Poblacion, 1979), p. 48.

11. Bourguignon, "Pobreza y Dualismo," p. 69.

12. Rakesh Mohan, *The People of Bogota: Who They Are, What They Earn, Where They Live*, World Bank Staff Working Paper no. 390 (Washington, D.C., 1980).

13. Mauricio Carrizosa, "Determinantes de los Ingresos y la Pobreza en Colombia" (Bogota: CEDE, Universidad de los Andes, 1971, processed).

14. In the human capital approach, education is a determinant of lifetime income. In Colombia it has been shown that education and age explain a large proportion of income differentials; therefore, education may be a good proxy for lifetime income.

15. François Bourguignon, "The Role of Education in the Urban Labor Market during the Process of Development" (Paper presented at the Sixth World Congress of the International Economics Association, August 1980, Mexico City, processed).

16. In Colombia, on the average, one income earner supports himself and about two more people. Therefore, the Col\$2,780 of 1978 would generate an income of close to Col\$926 per capita. If 65 percent is spent on food, the food expenditure amounts to about Col\$600 per month, which is between estimates C and D in Table 44. These two estimates seem the most realistic minimum of food expenditure levels.

17. The data for 1963–65 are based on figures reported in Rafael Isaza, "Ocupacion y Desocupacion en Bogota," in *Empleo y Desempleo* (Bogota: CEDE, Universidad de los Andes, 1968), pp. 123, 135. The data for 1974 and 1978 are based on tabulations of the EH-8E and EH-19 surveys of DANE. The denominator of the index is the percentage of employed nonfarm workers in the total number of employed persons.

18. In 1967, urban unemployment in Colombia was higher than in any other year between 1961 and 1980, and the economy grew at one of the lowest rates of that period.

19. This is not strictly an estimate of those actually malnourished. It is an estimate of the proportion of people who do not have an income that is adequate to cover their food and nutrition needs under existing food and consumption habits and prices.

6

Some Hypotheses on the Determinants of Changes in Income Distribution in Colombia

THE PURPOSE OF THIS RESEARCH PROJECT was to determine how the standard of living of various classes of the Colombian population had changed during the 1960s and 1970s. A similar effort had been carried out for the 1940s and 1950s in another publication.[1] No systematic effort has been made to determine empirically the causes of the changes in income distribution. This chapter, however, offers some hypotheses that may explain the observed changes and that may, in the future, be empirically tested.

Labor Force Trends in the Countryside

One of the most significant changes in Colombia in the 1960s was that the rural labor force ceased to grow.[2] As the demand for agricultural products continued to increase, rural labor productivity per capita began to improve markedly. In the 1960s, the lack of growth in the supply of labor in rural areas probably reduced the degrees of underemployment in agriculture, but in the 1970s the real income of agricultural laborers started to grow because of two mechanisms. First, agricultural prices increased somewhat more rapidly than the general price level, and small farmers and landless workers received part of this gain. Second, productivity per worker increased, as output expanded while the supply of labor contracted. Because landless laborers were the poorest group in Colombian society, their improved income led to a decrease in the proportion of families below the poverty line and to an improvement in the income distribution.

117

The improvement of wages in the countryside was also transmitted to unskilled workers in the cities. Migration from rural to urban areas is a function of rural-urban income differentials and urban unemployment rates. As rural incomes improved, rural-urban migration could only continue if wages in the cities also improved or unemployment decreased. The empirical evidence suggests both things occurred. The urban labor demand absorbed all the natural labor growth of both rural and urban areas, while also absorbing part of the pool of urban unemployed workers that existed at the end of the 1960s. This tight labor market in the countryside seems to have led to some decrease in the wage differential between agricultural laborers and urban unskilled workers, but the income data analyzed in previous chapters show that the earnings of unskilled urban workers also increased in real terms.

Despite gains in labor productivity in agriculture, labor demand did not decrease in the rural areas. In the first place, agricultural exports increased. The most dramatic case was that of coffee, the production of which almost doubled in the decade of the 1970s. This increased production required substantial investment in preparing land and planting the new coffee variety. The new variety (caturra) has increased the output per laborer, but during the time that the old plantations were being renewed and new lands prepared for caturra production, the demand for rural labor was high. Furthermore, coffee producers invested a high proportion of their windfall gains from the high world coffee prices of 1975–78 in renewing their plantations and planting caturra. In summary, the high investment in new coffee technology in the 1970s demanded much rural labor, and this was one determinant of higher rural wages.

Because world demand for coffee grows slowly, the expansion of coffee production could not continue after Brazil recovered from the 1975 frost. The increase in labor demand associated with the introduction of the caturra technology, therefore, cannot be expected to continue. The weakening of this component of rural labor demand might be expected to affect rural incomes negatively.

The export of cut flowers also grew extremely rapidly during the 1970s. This is an activity that makes intensive use of female labor. In the rural areas where flowers are grown for export, family incomes have increased substantially by the incorporation of women into the labor force.

Economic policy during the period of high coffee prices favored rural labor income in various ways. First, minimum wages in the countryside were increased rapidly when the labor market was tight. Second, part of the increases in world prices were passed on to coffee producers, in a country where most production is still in the hands of small and medium-size producers. Third, the supply of nonagricultural imported products was allowed to increase to avoid the increases in prices of consumer goods that would have occurred had rural incomes increased and import growth been restrained. During the coffee boom, Colombian industry was functioning at full capacity utilization, and a tight import policy would have led to rapid increases in the prices of nonfood consumer products.

During the 1970s, the export of illegal drugs (marijuana and cocaine) also increased dramatically. Such exports may have gone from negligible figures to about US$500 million in 1977–78.[3] Colombia became an important exporter of cocaine, but since the cocaine paste was not produced locally, but imported from Bolivia and Peru, this line of business only produced very high profits to a few underworld entrepreneurs and their laborers; it had little impact on labor demand. The industry was also capital-intensive; it used expendable airplanes, laboratories, ships, and armaments, but very little labor. While marijuana was grown in Colombia, most of the value added was produced in the United States where it was sold. The rural labor force involved in growing marijuana is small, located mostly in the non–coffee-producing north coast of the country, thus coincidentally increasing labor demand in an area where the coffee boom had little impact. In summary, the illegal drug exports of the 1970s probably had little impact on labor incomes, but they did produce some very high capital incomes for a very small group of people. This phenomenon probably helps to explain why the average incomes of the top 5 percent of the income distribution probably grew quite rapidly in the decade. In cities like Barranquilla and Medellin, there was indeed a feeling that much of the trade in luxury apartments and automobiles was dominated by people tainted by these illegal activities.

Labor Force Trends in the Cities

Although urban labor supply increased rapidly in the 1970s, economic growth was sufficiently rapid in labor-intensive sectors to absorb both the increase in the labor force and part of the high levels of unemployment common in the late 1960s. The decline in unemployment, especially among the poor, clearly reduced the proportion of families living below the poverty line. But the increasing participation of women in the labor force probably contributed even more to the improved welfare of the lower deciles of the population. The data from Cali show not only that women increased their labor force participation, but that the income of these additional unskilled workers grew at much higher rates than the average for all occupations.

Many of the changes in labor supply have to do with the decrease in the rate of population growth between the 1950s and the 1970s; that rate declined from about 3.3 percent to 2 percent a year. Even so, the labor force continued to grow rapidly in the 1970s because participation rates increased and the labor force had to absorb the postwar baby boom. The question that must now be addressed is what factors explain the rapid increase in labor demand in the 1970s.

Sectoral Growth in the 1970s

It is not easy to understand why labor demand grew so rapidly in Colombia in the 1970s. In fact, one report in 1970 had projected growing unemployment levels even on the assumption of rapid rates of economic growth.[4]

Some of the possible causes for a high labor demand in the countryside have been outlined earlier. It is more difficult to pinpoint the reasons why urban labor demand was able to absorb the natural rate of growth of the urban labor force, plus the rural people who migrated to the cities and part of the stock of those unemployed during the 1970s. Three factors may help to explain this phenomenon. For various reasons, sectors with low capital-output ratios grew faster than the sectors with high capital-output ratios; the latter grew faster in the 1960s. Some service sectors with low capital-labor ratios also grew rapidly. In the government sector, for example, the policy was to keep wages constant in real terms, or even to decrease them, while increasing the amount of coverage of services by increasing the number of employed people. This policy was followed in areas like education and the police. Finally, macroeconomic policy favored sectors with lower capital-labor ratios.

A series of economic policy reforms starting in 1967 seem to have contributed to a structural change in the economy that helped to create employment. In that year, the government initiated a policy of opening up the economy, which had various positive effects. The institution of a crawling peg, in which the exchange rate is devalued by a few cents against the dollar two or three times a week, eliminated both the overvaluation of the Colombian peso and the periodic exchange-rate crises common in the 1960s. This gradual approach to devaluation depoliticized the exchange rate, allowed a real depreciation of the Colombian peso between 1967 and 1975, and avoided the revaluation that would have occurred in a floating-exchange-rate regime when, after 1975, foreign exchange earnings increased dramatically because of temporarily high coffee prices.

The move toward a long-run equilibrium exchange rate encouraged labor-intensive exports and reduced the bias against agriculture created by import-substituting policies. The latter effect, well documented by Jorge Garcia, allowed the performance of the agricultural sector to improve.[5] Because agricultural production in Colombia is very labor intensive, this change in policy helps explain the improvement in agricultural incomes.

Another factor that increased the rural demand for labor was the technological change in coffee production. During the 1970s, the adoption of the new high-productivity caturra variety caused coffee production almost to double. Although this new technology produced more coffee per acre and per worker, its profitability led to large investments in new plantations and the preparation of land for these plantations. The rural demand for labor, therefore, grew rapidly during this investment boom. The government policy of transferring part of the high international coffee prices during the decade to the coffee growers assured them a cash flow for carrying out these investments.

Export subsidies and an adequate exchange rate stimulated production and exports of items like cut flowers, which generated substantial labor demand in the rural areas around Bogota, Medellin, and Cali.

In the cities, the labor-intensive sectors also appear to have grown more rapidly than those with high capital-labor ratios. Small industry seems to have grown more rapidly than large industry. Truck and bus transport, and other labor-intensive sectors, also grew more rapidly than the average. Within large industry, however, there is no clear evidence to show a faster growth of labor-intensive sectors.

In contrast, the elimination of import controls and periodic exchange-rate crises increased the degree of capital utilization in industry, and this clearly promoted employment growth. In the 1960s, there was excess capacity in industry because entrepreneurs would overinvest in imported capital equipment when the balance-of-payments situation was good, knowing that they would not be allowed to import when the balance of payments was negative. Furthermore, with import controls, an enterprise that could show excess capacity could convince the import authorities not to give licenses for capital equipment to competing industries or licenses to importers of competing foreign goods. The upward adjustment of the exchange rate between 1967 and 1973 also raised the prices of imported capital equipment and favored domestic labor. In addition, easier access to import licenses made possible a decrease in inventories of industrial inputs and spare parts. This phenomenon also lowered capital-output ratios.

In summary, the gradual move away from overvalued exchange rates in the 1970s probably favored employment, and this improved the income of the poor.

The Impact of the Supply of Education

The shifts in the middle of the income distribution were probably determined by the supply of education and inflation.

In the 1960s and 1970s, Colombia made a great effort to increase the supply of educated manpower. According to the *World Development Report 1980*, the number of children enrolled in primary school rose from 77 percent of the normal primary school age group in 1960 to 103 percent in 1977.[6] Progress in secondary school and university education was even more spectacular. The number of youths enrolled in secondary school went from 12 percent of the age group in 1960 to 39 percent in 1977, and the percentage of the population twenty to twenty-four years of age enrolled in higher education rose from 2 percent to 9 percent.

This increase in the supply of educated manpower had to lower the rate of return to education, and there is some empirical evidence to confirm this hypothesis. François Bourguignon reported earnings functions for various years in the decade 1965–75 and concluded that the returns to education declined significantly between the mid-1960s and the mid-1970s.[7] This was particularly true for university education. In relative terms, individuals with university education may have lost between 30 percent and 45 percent of the advantage they had during the 1960s over those who had completed only primary school. For secondary education, the corresponding relative loss was between 25 percent and 30 percent.[8] Using different data, Kugler, Reyes, and Gomez also identified the trend toward a decrease in the returns to education.[9]

The rapid increases in the supply of educated manpower may explain the sluggish growth in the real earnings of white-collar workers. The stagnation in the real income of this category of workers explains part of the loss of participation in total income of the middle-class deciles (seventh to ninth deciles) of the population.[10] The fact that these groups saw their relative position improve in the 1960s and deteriorate in the 1970s coincides with the trends in the rates of return to education.

Another factor that contributed to stagnant earnings and increased unemployment among educated workers in the 1970s was the slow growth of the government sector. Because government employs a large proportion of highly educated workers, a growth of government services should increase the demand for this type of labor and, therefore, also increase the real earnings of the middle class. From 1967 to 1971, central government expenditures, in real terms, on wages and salaries of government employees grew by 42 percent; from 1971 to 1980, however, such expenditures grew by only 7 percent. The consolidated central government sector (the various ministries, decentralized institutes, and central government-owned enterprises) had a less drastic, but still significant, decrease in the rate of growth of expenditures on wages and salaries. From 1967 to 1971, such expenditures grew by 52 percent in real terms, while, from 1971 to 1979, they grew by only 23 percent.

The Effect of Growing Inflation Rates on Income Distribution

The acceleration of inflation in the first part of the 1970s also had negative effects on white-collar employees and skilled workers in modern industry. From the late 1940s to the late 1960s, a process of collective bargaining was developed in Colombia, which led to the determination of wages in modern-sector enterprises on the basis of negotiated agreements signed for two-year periods.[11] This institutional framework determined that when the rate of inflation accelerated in the early 1970s, real wages started to decline because of a lag in the adjustment of wages to inflation.[12] By 1975, however, an institutional change had occurred and collective bargaining agreements were being negotiated every year. In the public sector, before 1975, wage increases required legislation to be passed by Congress, and such laws were passed only every two or three years; yearly increases began only in the middle of the 1970s. For these reasons, in both the private and the public sectors, real wages decreased when inflation accelerated.

Another institutional factor that affected real wages during a period of accelerating inflation was the practice of infrequently changing the minimum wage.[13] Since 1963, the minimum wage has been lower than the wage actually paid in the modern sector in the urban areas. Between 1963 and 1974, the minimum wage declined in real terms, and, when inflation accelerated in the early 1970s, the minimum wage was not used to avoid lags between negotiated wages and inflation. Starting in 1976, however, the minimum wage has been adjusted more frequently, and this has had some influence on wage bargaining agreements since unions and employees take into consideration the increase in the minimum wage when bargaining.

In summary, the institutional arrangements prevalent in the Colombian labor market in the 1960s were not well adapted to cope with an acceleration in inflation. When this happened, the real wages and salaries of modern sector workers suffered. In the urban traditional sector, where wage contracts either do not exist or are short term, wages kept up with inflation better.

But if institutional factors explain the decrease in real wages in the early 1970s, why did modern sector workers not recover lost ground during the rest of the decade? One possibility is that in all societies income differentials are very rigid and that, even if the underlying demand and supply conditions warrant a decrease in the differential between white-collar and unskilled workers, social traditions and social structure make such a change difficult. The acceleration of inflation, on the other hand, may have made such a change imperceptible, and, once made, underlying market forces made it impossible to return to the status quo ante.

The Disappearance of Dualism in the Labor Market

Another major structural change in the Colombian economy in the 1970s was the apparent fading of the dual economy characteristics of the labor market. In the 1960s, technological and labor market dualism appeared to be an important feature of the economy, and the two studies written in the decade that dealt with issues of income distribution used a dual economy model to analyze the trends in income distribution.

On the basis of data for the period 1958–65, Nelson, Schultz, and Slighton concluded that the "basic hypothesis is that the introduction of a modern sector on top of the traditional craft sector, and the widening of the productivity gap between the two, present the potential for a growing inequality of the distribution of income."[14] They had forecast that the major beneficiaries of this development were likely to be the members of the eighth and ninth deciles of the income distribution. In short, what is commonly identified as the "middle" and "lower-middle" class was expected to increase in relative size and increase its share of total income.

Exactly the opposite took place, however. This group's share of income declined in the 1970s and the real salaries of middle-class employees and skilled workers in modern industry decreased in some cases and increased little in other cases. One possible hypothesis is that the degree of dualism in the economy diminished.

The second study, by Urrutia and Berry, also hypothesized the existence of surplus labor and of traditional and modern sectors to explain the historical trend in income distribution in Colombia. This analysis anticipates that a worsening of the income distribution is particularly probable during the first part of the development process. Afterwards, when the economy emerges from the labor-surplus condition, the distribution is likely to improve.[15]

The recorded increase in agricultural wages in the 1970s would be consistent with the transition to a development phase with a less dualistic economy. It is possible then that as the economy emerged from the labor-surplus condition, dualism and imperfections in the labor market decreased.

The labor market studies carried out in Colombia before 1970 seem to offer substantial evidence of dualism. For example, Nelson, Schultz, and Slighton found that "the indirect evidence is very strong that the inequality of the distribution of wages outside agriculture has been widening in Colombia over the past fifteen years or so. Most of this change appears explicable in terms of a dual economy hypothesis."[16]

In the previous chapter, in contrast, a decreasing gap was discovered between the incomes of workers in the modern and traditional sectors and among workers with different skill levels. This would point to a decrease in dualism in the labor market. This trend is confirmed by a large set of research results that find no evidence of dualism in the labor market in the 1970s.

Recently, a number of studies have suggested that when a correction is made for skill level, earnings in the modern and traditional sectors are similar. In fact, Kugler, Reyes, and Gomez found that when they disaggregated the demand for labor between the modern and nonmodern sectors on the basis of size of establishment, public or private status, and other hiring and employment characteristics, there were income differences among sectors. Average wages in the modern sectors are higher than average wages or incomes in the nonmodern sectors. But when adjustment is made for sex, schooling, and experience, the difference in average labor income disappears. The study, therefore, concludes that in 1975 there was sufficient mobility and interaction of markets in Colombia to prevent intersector differentials in labor earnings in urban areas.[17]

Bourguignon reached the same conclusion in two recent studies.[18] In the first, which is based on 1974 data, he concluded that:

• Urban poverty is not limited to the traditional sector.

• The "residual" nature of the traditional sector seems to be far from a fact.

• It is not certain that the modern-traditional dichotomy corresponds to a real segmentation of the urban labor market.[19]

Finally, Fields also investigated the dualism hypothesis for the urban labor market of Bogota and concluded that it apparently is not highly segmented.[20]

In summary, a substantial number of investigators, using diverse methodologies, have concluded that the urban labor market in Colombia was quite competitive during the 1970s. The decreasing segmentation of the labor market would help explain some decrease in the dispersion of labor income in the urban areas during the decade. The decrease in segmentation was brought about by the elimination of excess labor in agriculture and by decreasing levels of urban unemployment and under-employment.

Import Substitution and Distribution

Another feature of the Colombian economy in the postwar period that was thought to contribute to the deterioration of income distribution was the import substitution policy. This hypothesis is at the core of the analysis by Nelson, Schultz, and Slighton. In another study, Urrutia and Berry also show that a period of worsening of the distribution of income in the 1950s coincided with the period of the most rapid import substitution.

The attempt to promote exports through exchange-rate policy starting in 1967 implied a moving away from import substitution policies. As the exchange rate became less overvalued, import controls were eased, and average import tariffs were decreased in the early 1970s. By 1973, most import licenses were being approved, and some imports were allowed in sectors that had been completely protected for several decades.

The gradual shift away from import substitution promoted some labor-intensive exports and decreased monopoly rents previously generated by quantitative import controls; this decreased the earnings of the top 5 percent of income recipients. As international coffee prices increased, different taxes on coffee exports were raised to avoid excessive increases in agricultural land rents. Thus, before 1975, the exchange rate was devalued in real terms to promote exports and employment.[21] After 1975, weekly nominal devaluations were continued, although the real exchange rate was allowed to revalue to some extent, despite very large surpluses in the current account of the balance of payments.

Exchange-rate policy, therefore, put downward pressure on income from capital invested in import-substituting industries before 1975; it also forced such industries to strike hard bargains with their workers, who, at the end of the 1960s, earned much higher wages than average. This policy probably dampened the growth of income of families in the two top deciles of the income distribution. Exchange-rate policy during the coffee and drug export booms after 1975 dampened the windfall gains of these exporters through different forms of export taxes and avoided a further deterioration of urban industrial wages by preventing an appreciation of the exchange rate that would have been too harsh on import-substituting industries. The gradual dismantling of import controls, however, kept profits in modern-sector industries at reasonable levels.

The Impact of Monetary and Credit Policy

During the 1970s, greater freedom was introduced in the capital market. It is hard to say what effect this policy had on income distribution.

This greater freedom, however, made credit available to individuals and small firms that could not give bankers impressive guarantees as collateral on their loans. At higher interest rates, bankers found these customers attractive, while when interest rates were controlled and there was excess demand for credit, bankers would ration credit to large customers, with good guarantees, to minimize risk and administrative costs. Small firms and medium-size commercial farmers benefited from liberalization because they could have cheaper and better access to institutional credit. Financial market liberalization, therefore, benefited these economic actors and decreased the profits of large modern-sector enterprises that had access to subsidized credit when such funds were being rationed. This effect of credit liberalization should improve income distribution.

Financial liberalization also led to higher interest rates on deposits. This would presumably benefit high-income families, because they are the ones who have higher rates of saving. The impact on income distribution of higher interest rates on deposits is, however, more complicated. Persons with high incomes in Colombia (the top 5 percent of the income distribution) had access to the international financial market and to the curb market; therefore, real interest rates did not increase for their investments. The higher interest rates probably did increase the returns to capital of middle-class families and compensated to a small extent the low growth in real labor income of this sector of the population.

To the extent that a freer capital market brought about a better allocation of credit and helped bring down capital-output ratios, financial liberalization also may have contributed to greater employment growth and to an improvement in the incomes of low-income workers. In summary, it is not at all clear that higher interest rates benefited the richest groups in society.

Many people in Colombia identified financial liberalization with income concentration through high profits for financial intermediaries owned by a small group of people. In 1982, however, several of the fastest growing financial groups collapsed; their owners went to jail, and it became clear that the profits of the financial sector, after deductions for bad debts, were not terribly impressive. Although substantial research on the impact on income distribution of greater competition and fast growth in the financial sector is needed, the assumption that many people in Colombia have made—namely, that financial liberalization concentrates income—should not be accepted uncritically.

The Impact of Fiscal Policy

In Colombia, surprisingly, fiscal policy may have some positive impact on income distribution. Urrutia and Berry offered some evidence suggesting that in the 1960s the tax system was slightly progressive and that government expenditures were redistributive.[22] For example, the income of the first decile of the economically active population was twice as high after taxes, government expenditures, and transfers as before, while the share of the top decile was reduced from 48 percent to about 42 percent.[23]

In his study of the incidence of government expenditures, Selowsky concluded that in education, health, and public services such as water and electricity, government programs benefit the poor in a more than proportional way.[24] The improvement in public service levels in the poor barrio of Cali explained in Chapter 3 confirms this.

In 1974, after these studies were made, however, the Colombian fiscal system was significantly reformed to make it even more progressive. A thorough and ambitious tax reform was carried out to make taxes more redistributive and to increse the share of government expenditure in the GNP.[25] Furthermore, the Development Plan of 1975 determined a shift in government expenditure toward programs that would directly benefit the poorer half of the population. The proportion of expenditures on education was increased, and ambitious nutrition and integrated rural development plans were initiated.[26]

Although for this research project we attempted to evaluate the impact of some of these new programs on poverty, it still is too early to tell whether they have been as effective as originally planned. There is some evidence, however, that the nutrition plan has been effective in the department of Cauca. Statistically significant evidence shows that for similar populations there are fewer undernourished children in areas where the plan has operated than in those with no program.[27]

Table 58. *Labor Income as a Percentage of* GDP *in Various Sectors,* 1962–78
(current prices)

Year	Agricultural sector	Manufacturing industry	Construction	Trade	Government services
1962	33.9	36.3	71.4	19.5	100.0
1963	35.6	36.5	73.6	18.3	100.0
1964	30.5	38.1	73.8	18.3	100.0
1965	34.3	38.1	74.4	18.3	100.0
1966	32.3	37.8	75.6	18.3	100.0
1967	32.1	38.9	77.4	18.3	100.0
1968	30.2	40.1	78.1	21.5	100.0
1969	31.3	39.9	81.1	21.7	100.0
1970	30.1	41.8	80.6	18.9	100.0
1971	29.7	40.8	78.7	18.6	100.0
1972	27.1	40.2	75.7	16.2	100.0
1973	23.9	35.2	73.7	14.0	100.0
1974	25.5	30.4	73.9	11.9	100.0
1975	23.8	31.2	74.9	12.1	100.0
1976	21.1	31.6	74.5	10.7	100.0
1977	22.9	31.6	73.8	10.9	100.0
1978	25.3	30.9	73.0	12.9	100.0

Source: Banco de la Republica national accounts.

In summary, redistribution through the fiscal system may have been a factor in the improvement in the income distribution after the tax and public expenditure reforms of 1974–75.

Distribution of Income from Capital

The reduction in the dispersion of urban labor income did not lead to an improvement in the distribution of urban income because of an apparent increase in the income share claimed by capital. The national accounts show this increase in capital income as a proportion of national income (see Table 58). This indicator does not really reflect the share of capital because it includes the incomes of small farmers and self-employed workers, which consist mostly of earnings from labor. Because the incomes of smallholders and self-employed workers in cities rose faster than the overall average in the 1970s, part of the apparent increase in the share of capital as shown in the national accounts was due to increases in labor income of small capitalists.

The apportioning of the gross domestic product (GDP) between labor and capital in the Colombian national accounts is fraught with methodological problems. It is clearly not realistic for the labor share in the trade sector to be at 10 percent, as shown in Table 58 for the 1970s. In Colombia, commerce is dominated by small family shops, and one would not expect 90 percent of GDP in the sector to be generated by capital. I do not believe statistical data on labor and capital share as calculated in Colombia have any value, and for that reason have not used this data source in this study.

Nevertheless, since many of the salary and wage series show lower growth rates than the national per capita income series, it might be concluded that the share of capital in national income increased somewhat. Because the wealthiest 20 percent of all urban families receive most of the capital income, excluding the imputed rental value of housing, an increase in the share of capital would tend to intensify the concentration of income.[28] There is, however, no reliable information on trends in income from capital available.

Conclusion

Although the empirical analysis of income trends in Colombia during the last two decades is a difficult task, two conclusions can be drawn. First, the overall distribution of income may have improved at the end of the 1970s. Second, it appears that absolute poverty was reduced, because the incomes of poor families rose during the 1970s at a rate matching or exceeding that of per capita income.

An independent study of malnutrition by Mohan, Wagner, and Garcia concludes that malnutrition decreased in Bogota and Cali between 1973 and 1978.[29] That study reports that probably 25 percent of the cities' population was undernourished because of low income in 1973 and only 12 percent in 1978.

Data by occupations also confirm the evidence on increases in the real incomes of the poorest groups. Real agricultural daily wages increased in the 1970s, especially during the latter half of the decade. The real wages of construction workers and other unskilled urban workers also increased. Wages of blue-collar and white-collar workers in the manufacturing industry rose at a slower rate. Although the total income of industrial workers, including employee benefits, seems to have risen between 1965 and 1980, the growth rate was lower than that of national per capita income, which implies a decline in the relative position of this group in the distribution of income. The situation of white-collar workers, and of the middle class in general, is even less encouraging. The absolute level of their real income may have declined, and unquestionably they suffered a loss in relative economic status.

These negative findings on the incomes of certain groups of urban workers may be corrected partially when family income is considered. The reduction in unemployment and the increase in the participation of females in the labor force may have increased family income, even if income per worker did not increase for these groups of society.

Because the incomes of the wealthiest families probably rose at least as rapidly as national per capita income, as did the income of poor families, the relative position of the so-called middle class clearly worsened. In the years before 1964, in contrast, that class benefited most from the economic development process. The sharp change in the relative position of this group has profound political implications.

Finally, while in most developing countries the so-called middle class has great influence on policy, the democratic nature of Colombian politics seems to give this class less weight in decisionmaking. Since elections have to be won, government programs and subsidies do not benefit exclusively the top three deciles of the income distribution, and economic policy is not always geared to favor the modern urban sectors. Politics, therefore, may have something to do with the improvement of the Colombian income distribution in the 1970s.

Slow income growth for middle-class workers, however, can lead to frustration in a politically strategic group of society. One optimistic conclusion to this study could be that the wage differentials in favor of middle-class workers were adjusted in the 1970s, and that in the future the differences in income growth among different classes will be less marked. Income distribution would improve through movement of people from low-income to higher-income occupations.

Notes to Chapter 6

1. Miguel Urrutia and Albert Berry, *La Distribucion del Ingreso en Colombia* (Medellin: Editorial la Carreta, 1975).

2. The number of persons employed in agriculture increased only from 2,087,949 in 1951 to 2,509,428 in 1964. This figure decreased to 1,546,517 in the 1973 census.

3. There are few serious estimates of the drug trade. These figures come from the only academic publication on the subject. Because the authors assume rather high figures for the capital flight in 1977, when there appeared to be, on the contrary, large illegal influxes of illegal capital, I would guess the drug trade was even smaller. See Roberto Junquito and Carlos Caballero, "Illegal Trade Transactions and the Underground Economy of Colombia," in Vito Tanzi (ed.), *The Underground Economy of Colombia in the United States and Abroad* (Lexington, Mass.: Lexington Books, 1982).

4. International Labour Organisation (ILO), *Hacia el Pleno Empleo* (Geneva, 1970).

5. See Jorge Garcia, "The Impact of Exchange Rate and Commercial Policy on Incentives to Agriculture in Colombia: 1953–58" (Washington, D.C.: International Food Policy Research Institute, November 1980; processed). The rate of the growth of agriculture has been as follows:

1955–60	2.3	1970–75	4.0
1960–65	2.1	1975–80	5.1
1965–70	4.1		

Also see La Economia Colombiana en la Decada de los Ochenta (Bogota: Fedesarrollo, 1979), p. 128; and Cuentas Nacionales 1970–79 y Estimacion PIB 1980 (Bogota: Banco de la Republica, 1981).

6. Because children younger and older than those from the bracket defined as containing school-age children can go to school, the children in school can exceed the number of children in the primary-school–age bracket. See World Development Report 1980 (New York: Oxford University Press, 1980).

7. François Bourguignon, "The Role of Education in the Urban Labor Market during the Process of Development: The Case of Colombia," (Paper presented at the Sixth World Congress of the International Economics Association, August 1980, Mexico City; processed).

8. Ibid., p. 11.

9. Bernardo Kugler, Alvaro Reyes, and Maria Isabel de Gomez, Education y Mercado de Trabajo Urbano en Colombia: Una Comparacion entre Sectores Moderno y no Moderno, monograph 10 (Bogota: Corporacion Centro Regional de Poblacion, 1979).

10. If the middle class is classified in terms of education, the size of that class would have increased and it would dominate more deciles of the income distribution.

11. For the development of this process, see Miguel Urrutia, The Development of the Colombian Labor Movement (New Haven: Yale University Press, 1969).

12. The rate of growth of the national consumer price index for employees was as follows:

		1970–71	10.1
1961–62	5.5	1971–72	13.2
1962–63	24.5	1972–73	19.6
1963–64	15.7	1973–74	23.3
1964–65	3.8	1974–75	22.1
1965–66	16.8	1975–76	20.1
1966–67	8.9	1976–77	31.3
1967–68	7.6	1977–78	18.9
1968–69	7.0	1978–79	23.9
1969–70	7.3	1979–80	24.9

13. The dates of changes in the minimum wage and its level in real terms (1969=100) are as follows:

August 1962	134.6	August 1976	90.3
January 1963	184.4	January 1977	101.9
July 1969	100.0	August 1977	84.3
April 1972	98.7	November 1977	106.3
December 1973	96.8	May 1978	107.5
November 1974	107.3	January 1979	131.0
		January 1980	131.7

See Coyuntura Economica, April 1979 and April 1980.

14. Richard Nelson, T. Paul Schultz, and Robert L. Slighton, Structural Change in a Developing Economy; Colombia's Problems and Prospects (Princeton, N.J.: Princeton University Press, 1971).

15. Urrutia and Berry, La Distribucion del Ingreso en Colombia, pp. 21–22.

16. Nelson, Schultz, and Slighton, Structural Change in a Developing Economy, p. 153.

17. Urban areas are defined as cities with population exceeding 30,000. See Kugler, Reyes, and Gomez, *Educacion y Mercado de Tabajo Urbano en Colombia.*

18. François Bourguignon, "Pobreza y Dualismo en el Sector Urbano de las Economias en Desarrollo: El Caso de Colombia," *Desarrollo y Sociedad,* no. 1 (January 1979); and Bourguignon, "The Role of Education."

19. Bourguignon, "Pobreza y Dualismo," p. 69.

20. Gary Fields, *How Segmented Is the Bogota Labor Market?* World Bank Staff Working Paper no. 434 (Washington, D.C., January 1980).

21. Urrutia and Berry, *La Distribucion del Ingreso en Colombia,* p. 32.

22. Ibid., p. 202.

23. Ibid., pp. 208–09.

24. Marcelo Selowsky, *Who Benefits from Government Expenditure? A Case Study of Colombia* (New York: Oxford University Press, 1979).

25. For an evaluation of this tax reform, see Malcolm Gillis and Charles E. McLure, *La Reforma Tributaria de 1974* (Bogota: Banco Popular, 1977).

26. Expenditures on education went up from 13 percent of the total central government expenditure in 1970 to 18 percent in 1980.

27. Mario Ochoa, "El Plan Nacional de Alimentacion y Nutricion en el Cauca" (Bogota: Fedesarrollo, 1980; processed).

28. Philip Musgrove, *Consumer Behavior in Latin America* (Washington, D.C.: Brookings Institution, 1978), chapter 2.

29. Rakesh Mohan, M. W. Wagner, and Jorge Garcia, *Measuring Urban Malnutrition and Poverty: A Case Study of Bogota and Cali, Colombia,* World Bank Staff Working Paper no. 447 (Washington, D.C., 1981).

References

Ayala, Ulpiano, and Nohra Rey de Marulanda, *Empleo y Pobreza*. Bogota: Centro de Estudios para el Desarrollo Economico (CEDE) Universidad de los Andes, July 1978.

Bejarano, J. A. "Crecimiento, Distribucion y Politica Economica." Paper presented at the Congreso de Economistas de la Universidad Nacional, Melgar, May 1980. Processed.

Berry, Albert, and Alfonso Padilla. *La Distribucion de Ingresos Provenientes de la Agricultura en Colombia, 1960.* CID, Universidad Nacional, Documentos de Trabajo, January/March 1970.

Berry, Albert, and Ronald Soligo. *Economic Policy and Income Distribution in Colombia.* Boulder, Colo.: Westview Press, 1980.

Bourguignon, François. "Pobreza y Dualismo en el Sector Urbano de las Economias en Desarrollo: El Caso de Colombia." *Desarrollo y Sociedad*, January 1979.

––––––. "The Role of Education in the Urban Labor Market During the Process of Development: The Case of Colombia." Paper presented at the Sixth World Congress of the International Economics Association, Mexico City, August 1980. Processed.

Cordoba, Polibio. "Analisis Econometrico de Distribucion de Ingresos." Departamento Administrativo Nacional de Estadistica (DANE), July 1972.

DANE, *Boletin Mensual de Estadistica*. Various issues.

––––––. *Encuesta Nacional de Hogares 1970.* Bogota, 1971.

––––––. *Encuesta Nacional de Hogares: Fuerza de Trabajo 1971.* Bogota, July 1976.

––––––. *Encuesta Nacional de Hogares 1974: Demografia, Educacion y Fuerza de Trabajo en Bogota, Medellin, Cali, Barranquilla.* Bogota, 1976.

––––––. *Encuesta Nacional de Hogares 1972.* Bogota, December 1977.

––––––. *Encuesta Nacional de Hogares: Fuerza de Trabajo en Cabeceras Municipales 1974.* Bogota, 1977.

_____. *Encuesta Nacional de Hogares 1975: Fuerza de Trabajo en Bogota, Barranquilla, Cali, Bucaramanga, Medellin, Pasto, Manizales.* Bogota, 1977.

Departamento Nacional de Planeacion, *Para Cerrar la Brecha.* Bogota: Banco de la Republica, 1975.

Fields, Gary. *How Segmented Is the Bogota Labor Market?* World Bank Staff Working Paper no. 434. Washington, D.C., January 1980.

Garcia, Jorge. "La Programacion Industrial y el Arancel Externo Comun: Un Impuesto al Sector Agricola del Grupo Andino." *Coyuntura Economica,* July 1981.

_____. "The Impact of Exchange Rate and Commercial Policy on Incentives to Agriculture in Colombia: 1953–58." Washington, D.C.: International Food Policy Research Institute, November 1980. Processed.

Gillis, Malcolm, and Charles E. McLure. *La Reforma Tributaria de 1974.* Bogota: Banco Popular, 1977.

International Labour Organisation (ILO). *Hacia el Pleno Empleo.* Geneva, 1970.

Isaza, Rafael, and Francisco Ortega. *Encuestas Urbanas de Empleo y Desempleo.* Bogota: CEDE Universidad de los Andes, 1969.

Isaza, Rafael. "Ocupacion y Desocupacion en Bogota." In *Empleo y Desempleo en Colombia.* Bogota: CEDE, Universidad de los Andes, 1968.

Jaramillo, Helena. "Determinants of Income Differentials after Migration." New Haven: Yale University, 1978. Processed.

Kugler, Bernardo, Alvaro Reyes, and Maria Isabel de Gomez. *Educacion y Mercado de Trabajo Urbano en Colombia: Una Comparacion entre Sectores Moderno y no Moderno,* monograph 10. Bogota: Corporacion Centro Regional de Poblacion, 1979.

McKay, Harrison, and others. "Improving Cognitive Ability in Chronically Deprived Children." *Science,* vol. 200, April 21, 1978.

Mohan, Rakesh. *People of Bogota: Who They Are, What They Earn, Where They Live.* World Bank Staff Working Paper no. 390. Washington, D.C., 1980.

Mohan, Rakesh and Nancy Hartline. *The Poor of Bogota: Who They Are, What They Do, Where They Live.* World Bank Staff Working Paper no. 635. Washington, D.C., 1984.

Mohan, Rakesh, M. W. Wagner, and Jorge Garcia. *Measuring Urban Malnutrition and Poverty: A Case Study of Bogota and Cali, Colombia.* World Bank Staff Working Paper no. 447. Washington, D.C., 1981.

Musgrove, Philip. *Consumer Behavior in Latin America.* Washington, D.C.: Brookings Institution, 1978.

Musgrove, Philip, and Robert Ferber. "Finding the Poor." *Review of Income and Wealth,* vol. 24, September 1978.

_____. "Identifying the Urban Poor: Characteristics of Poverty Households in Bogota, Medellin, and Lima." *Latin American Research Review,* vol. 14, no. 2, 1979.

Nelson, Richard, T. Paul Schultz, and Robert L. Slighton. *Structural Change in a Developing Economy: Colombia's Problems and Prospects.* Princeton, N.J.: Princeton University Press, 1971.

Ochoa, Mario. "El Plan Nacional de Alimentacion y Nutricion en el Cauca." Bogota: Fedesarrollo, 1980. Processed.

Okhawa, Kazuchi, and Gustav Ranis. "On Phasing." Paper presented to the Conference on Japan's Historical Development Experience and Contemporary Developing Countries, Tokyo, 1978.

Prieto, Rafael, Bill Hanneson, and Marco Reyes. *Estudio Agronomico de la Hoya del Rio Suarez*. Bogota: Centro de Estudios para el Desarrollo Economico (CEDE)–Corporacion Autonoma Regional de la Sabana (CAR), 1965.

Prieto, Rafael, and others. *Fuentes y Usos de Recursos Financieros en el Sector Agropecuario de Colombia*. Bogota: Banco de la Republica, 1976.

Prieto, Rafael, "Gasto e Ingreso Familiar Urbano en Colombia." *Ensayos ECIEL*, no. 4, August 1977.

Ranis, Gustav. "Distribucion del Ingreso y Crecimiento en Colombia." *Desarrollo y Sociedad*, no. 3, January 1980.

Sandoval, Clara Elsa de, and Miguel Urrutia. "Distribucion del Ingreso Proveniente de la Actividad Agropecuaria en Colombia." Bogota: Fedesarrollo, November 1980. Processed.

Selowsky, Marcelo. *Who Benefits from Government Expenditure? A Case Study of Colombia*. New York: Oxford University Press, 1979.

Urrutia, Miguel. *The Development of the Colombian Labor Movement*. New Haven, Conn.: Yale University Press, 1969.

Urrutia, Miguel, and Albert Berry. *La Distribucion del Ingreso en Colombia*. Medellin: Editorial La Carreta, 1975.

Weisner, Guillermo. "Cien Años de Desarrollo Historico de los Precios de la Tierra en Bogota." *Revista Camara de Comercio de Bogota*, nos. 41 and 42. Bogota: Corporacion Centro Regional de Poblacion, 1980.

World Bank, *World Development Report 1980*. New York: Oxford University Press, 1980.

Index

Absolute poverty, 6, 70, 93, 94, 102, 113, 130
Agricultural production, 74, 76, 117–119, 121
Agriculture: development and, 12; technology and, 7, 118, 121. *See also* Income distribution, agricultural; Labor force, rural; Real wages, agricultural; Wages, landless agricultural/rural landowner/unskilled rural
Agudelo Villa, Hernando, 4
Altimir, Oscar, 94
ANIF. *See* National Association of Financial Institutions
Automobile sales, 46, 52, 119

Balance of payments, 121, 126
Banco de la Republica, 76–77
Bejarano, J. A., 4
Berry, Albert, 4, 5, 18, 74, 77, 124, 126, 128
Bourguignon, François, 94, 97, 122, 125
Brazil, 118

Cali (Colombia), 6, 19, 25, 55–70, 71n
Capital equipment, 121
Capital income, 9, 73, 76, 77, 119, 129–30
Capital market, 127–128
Capital-output ratios, 120, 122, 127
Carrizosa, Mauricio, 97
Caturra, 118, 121
CEDE. *See* Centro de Estudios para el Desarrollo Economico
Censuses, 5, 74, 76, 77, 115n

Centro de Estudios para el Desarrollo Economico (CEDE), 74, 76, 102
Cocaine, 119
Coffee: prices, 7, 118, 121, 126; production, 7, 13, 16, 118–19, 121. *See also* Caturra
Colombian Central Bank, 74
Communications, 17, 98
Concentration index, 104, 113
Consigna (Bogota), 3
Construction workers, 9, 18–25, 55, 67, 68, 97, 98, 106, 107, 130
Consumer goods, 64, 119. *See also* Automobile sales
Consumer price index, 102, 132n
Consumption levels, 59, 61, 62, 64
Credit, 74, 77, 127

DANE. *See* Departmento Administrativo Nacional de Estadistica
Democracy, 3, 131
Departmento Administrativo Nacional de Estadistica (DANE), 12, 13, 16, 18, 25, 28, 34, 53n, 67, 73, 74, 85, 88, 96, 97, 102, 107; Monthly Survey of Manufacturing, 28, 29
Development. *See* Agriculture, development and; Economic policies; "Para Cerrar la Brecha"
Development Plan (1975), 128
Domestic industry, 64
Domestic service workers, 18, 76, 77, 97
Drug exports, 119, 127
Dual economy, 12, 124–26

The full range of World Bank publications, both free and for sale, is described in the *Catalog of Publications*; the continuing research program is outlined in *Abstracts of Current Studies*. Both booklets are updated annually; the most recent edition of each is available without charge from the Publications Distribution Unit, Department B, The World Bank, 1818 H Street, N.W., Washington, D.C. 20433, U.S.A.

Miguel M. Urrutia, formerly a consultant at The World Bank, is vice-rector, Development Studies Division, at the United Nations University in Tokyo. .